ALABASTER

MOMENTS

FEELING SAFE, SECURE, AND RESPECTED

SHARON JONES, LMFT

ISBN: 978-0-578-26846-0

Book production by MysticqueRose Publishing Services LLC

THE POURING OF ALABASTER

A Poem to My Ancestors'

Dynasty

I am the descendant

Daughter from a dynasty

Circumstances and situations

Want to destroy my legacy

I believed in my spirit

Knowing I am free

Guided by the marvelous light

Of truth and unity

Not allowing the oppressor

To detain the true me

Owning my power

Over my mind, spirit, and body

Seeing the chains as only

Minor distractions to bind me

I hear the powerful

Voices of my ancestors

Hiding from view

Saying they want to find me

You are not lost

We are walking with thee

You are safe and protected

Keep walking in dignity

Do not allow others to transfer

Hate within your energy

Do not let them

Tell you who to be

Do not allow them

To enter your dynasty

DEDICATION

We Exist Because of God

I dedicate this book to the being of infinite wisdom and intelligence, God. He is my creator, the author of my DNA, the designer of my blueprint. In Him I live and have my being. He is the one who orders my steps and illuminates my pathway with wisdom for action.

I humbly send and give thanks each day for an opportunity to touch and contribute to the lives of others. I honor all of my ancestors, my grandmother (Mama Honey), my parents, siblings, family members, friends, and those looking to breathe easier in life with a powerful spiritual connection and a marvelous spirit that leads them to experiencing magnificent encounters. A very special dedication to my brother, Michael J. Jones, who was and still is the "block" of our family. The little boy from Jim River who flowed just like the water around the rocks and fulfilled his dreams as a military officer. I honor him with this book and salute him for a life well lived and a job well done! We miss you in the earth dimension. You led the charge for Alabaster Moments, always smiling, believing, and living great moments while enjoying life in spite of the situations you faced.

I salute the small rural town of Coushatta, Louisiana, and speak words of massive blessings, protection, restoration, hope, and favor over all the souls living in that amazing place. I pray my hometown be filled with the spirit of God's power, amazing wonder, healing, transformation, innovation, restoration, and splendor. May unlimited blessings shower down from the heavens and open up great opportunities for all who live in and enter the town. I dedicate this book to anyone who has stopped living their life and is just existing, unable to find joy and happiness because of pain, grief, loss, physical illness, mental distress, sadness, and depression.

OVERVIEW

This book is about pausing and reflecting on your life and taking an inventory of your life's moments. After doing so, you will become aware of how you are living. Are you taking time to see and experience great moments and utilizing those moments as motivation to live from a place of power, strength, and might? Moments can empower us if we become aware of the important healing benefits of the special instances that have shaped and molded our lives. When we cultivate awareness, develop a plan, and set up a process to explore quality moments in life, we are able to continuously restore our mind, body, and spirit. The carving out of times of awe provides space for the integration of a healthy flow, creating a powerful release into our lives.

Alabaster Moments are healthy, restorative, and/or intentional ~~moments~~ experiences of spending therapeutic time releasing, rejuvenating, relaxing, healing, and creating true renewal. The spirit of this book is transformation, and it flows from the holy sacred book that gives life. I have embraced this Holy Book since I was a child growing up in humble beginnings. You will find in this holy sacred book many words that give hope and a better perspective of the way we live.

The story that inspires this book is the story in the Bible about the woman carrying an alabaster box filled with valuable, expensive perfumes. She entered the room, unwelcomed, where Jesus was dining. In his presence, she broke the box open, anointing him, and fragrance filled the room.

This woman had been judged by others and was presumed to have lived a life of sin. She was broken by her life situations and experiences, but she set up this moment in time for a better life—one of value instead of shame, one in which she was loved and respected rather than ridiculed and judged. She set up an environment of release to give the most valuable possession she had in life—the fragrances she carried in that alabaster box. When she released the fragrance in the box, it changed the room. Courage and forgiveness of self came forth, and fear was replaced with potential and possibility. This moment shaped and affected everyone in the room.

This was a powerful release of all that she was carrying in the box and throughout her life. This was a divine, sacred encounter that transformed and upgraded her life story. Her story is now timeless and has been told from generation to generation.

It is my belief that instants occur that empower us, open our awareness, give us hope and strength, and open us up to more possibilities in life. These encounters can provide healing and restoration, just as the woman's alabaster box brought release and transformation.

Alabaster Moments are valuable and sacred encounters that become agents of change that ignite transformation during situations in which you are broken or your light begins to flicker or become dim. Alabaster Moments (AM) help us to believe, to live great moments, and enjoy life in spite of the situations we are faced with.

PREFACE

I am Sharon Jones, and my early life was shaped by very humble beginnings. I grew up in a small home with no inside amenities. I did not have my own bedroom or personal space. The area was isolated and far away from other homes and families. The roads were bumpy, dusty, and unpaved. Despite this, I was aware of the positivity in my surroundings that fostered hope and gratitude. There were many cows in the pasture on the left of the house. To the right of the house was a small fig tree with tasty figs. In the back of the house was a beautiful, healthy, vibrant, large pecan tree, and running at the back of the property was a peaceful flowing river.

Our family was happy even though our mindset was focused on survival and scarcity. Our grandmother, Mama Honey, lived in the home with us. One of my earliest memories is of her preparing special treats for us, such as wrapping shoeboxes with colorful decorative paper and placing cracked pecans, fruit, and candy inside. Sometimes she would even add an apple or an orange. She would make sure all of us children had a decorative box. It was such a special treat.

I remember so vividly the flourishing pecan tree being so alive and vibrant, producing pecans each year, contributing so greatly to our lives. We were able to sell the pecans from the tree for money to buy food, clothing, and the things we needed to survive. The tree was a very faithful provider and was a major lifeline for me and my family. The decorative shoeboxes and the giving pecan tree have greatly molded and shaped my life.

Growing up in this special place called Jim River, which was filled with beautiful nature, agricultural fields, animals, a peaceful, serene, flowing water stream, and a river in the back of the house. The house had a chimney, and we roasted sweet potatoes in the fireplace. We picked pecans daily with our grandmother and enjoyed watching the dust as cars drove on the road.

I remember the fierce thunderstorms and flashes of lightning. I remember the rain tapping heavily on the metal roof. We did not have a lot of money, but I'll forever cherish those memories. Oh, such memories of a caring mother, father, and grandmother, and a brother who was strong, resilient, and motivated.

I was born in Shreveport, Louisiana, and raised in Coushatta, Louisiana. I now live in California. I am a licensed psychotherapist of the healing arts and a spiritual life coach. I have worked for over twenty-five years supplying an atmosphere and environment for recovery, building hope and comfort to many clients in need of transformation in their lives, utilizing creative practices that promote healing, wellness, coping, and personal change. I believe that reintroducing positive moments and experiences in life creates an anchor to build upon and reset the mind, body, and spirit. When speaking of these positive situations, I call them Alabaster Moments.

This book has been stirring in my spirit for years. It is a message of healing to the world. Together, we will learn the magnificent power of relaxing and encouraging times. We will learn how to show and build simple, healthy practices into your life, and recall points in time to promote appreciation, humility, balance, and wellness, as well as the harmony of mind, body, and spirit. It is through this message that freedom for self and others will happen. This book is authentic and expresses my sincere desire to help others, to empower them to unpack and release the weight of all their problems and bad situations, to become more intentional in living from a place of optimism, to take back their power in setting up great moments of glory, and to no longer wait for someone else to rescue them.

This book is my message of healing, living better moments on Earth, and contributing to the world. Through this message, I intend to shift perspectives and activate relief and the release of the pressures in life.

If you feel that your life is broken and has malfunctioned, the broken pieces can become building blocks to greatness, positive actions, and change. Imagine we are made of alabaster, which gives us the strength to mold and shape our lives to greatness. Think back to those wonderful memories that you want to relive that speak great joy and happiness during a time of calm, goodness, and serenity. Those times that give the feeling of "all is well," an abundant life, and a fulfilled spirit. Moments filled with unconditional love that can be compared to the rising of a beautiful sunset; the pouring of rain; visiting a beautiful, peaceful place with magnificent hills and mountains, glorious, vibrant wildflowers growing free; sitting by the massive and powerful ocean; having a wonderful, tasty meal; or meeting someone who has wisdom that encourages and inspires you to want to learn more, who shares hopeful and positive words that speak to your inner spirit.

CONTENTS

INTRODUCTION

The time you spend for yourself is the most important time in your life

–Sharon Jones

FLOWING FROM MY HEART

I affirm that the words from my mouth and the meditation from my heart be acceptable in the sight of God, our Creator.

It has been said that out of the heart comes the issues of life. In my heart, I realize it is an honor to live on earth—to learn, grow, experience life, and help others. I truly believe that it is my calling to help others live better by seeing their full potential and the size of their worth. I appreciate the opportunity and honor to live on Earth, the great creation of God. In spite of everything that I have experienced on this journey, I still say "God over everything." I know the benefit of aligning with God. I have learned to listen to His voice and to allow Him to direct my pathways.

Even when my mind goes into a negative, defeated frequency, such as telling me "This is going to be a bad day." Or "Why bother to author a book?" After all, I come from humble beginnings, and that did impact my confidence and self-esteem, making me feel less than. However, God has shown up with wonder, amazement, and transformative, infinite wisdom. His spirit has led me to the right thinking, to positive thinking. The experiences of awe that He has given me have been more precious than gold, rubies, diamonds, or any material possessions. My heart, mind, and spirit continue to recall special points in time filled with stories and memories of comebacks, restoration, and transformation.

Early in life, I have seen how God can make something out of nothing, and across my divine path, I have experienced many extraordinary encounters of helping, empowering others, and more. I met those wanting and in need of an awakening to new narratives and a reshaping of their belief system. Those wanting more of a spirit of happiness, optimism, and good times. Those who want more sacred, positive, and vividly defining experiences in their lives.

It is through the sharing of meaningful information and stories that we begin to learn and create memories to motivate and guide us through life. Think of the memories that you look back upon that have refocused, refreshed, and helped to change the way you feel. Think of how these times have built personal resiliency to help strengthen the present moment and have motivated you to restart and move forward with gratitude and hope for a bright future. This book is for the person who finds themself in a place of hurting, fear, panic, anxiety, indecision, being looked down upon due to life choices and being judged, talked about and counted out in life.

In this book, I appreciate the ability to bring out the great moments in my life. So, too, do I appreciate *your* ability to bring out the great moments in your life. I hope my words comfort and inspire you to honor the potency of being aware and seeing with the lens of that which is good. I encourage each of you to show, embrace, and live by spiritual truths to build daily divine restoration, renewal, and transformation. Use these spiritual truths to embrace, revive, and recharge your spirit daily. Some of the spiritual truths are love, appreciation, honesty, and faith, as well as living abundantly and valuing life.

I am authoring this book to increase the world's sense of healing and restoration of mind, body, and spirit. I believe when we reset the way we perceive ourselves and our situations, we move towards a new beginning, a second chance and better response to circumstances. If we never reset our lives, we are stuck in that place of feeling alone, unfocused, and unwilling to act. As we feel better, we begin to radiate good positive energy to others and the world.

I have personally seen the strength and effectiveness of aligning our energy to positive thoughts and actions, being positive, and focusing on positive thoughts and actions. Concentrating on the bright periods in life produces amazing feelings of being alive, vibrancy, and goodness.

It is important to always reach and strive for the newness of life, which is a higher vibration of motivational energy. In my opinion, it is very important to always place the sacred first by finding spiritual truths to guide and renew our lives. As we move in sacred energy, we can breathe easier and find purpose in our hearts. We can walk in the power of our Creator, who has modeled the way. When we develop and engage in upstream preventive strategies—such as unplugging from electronics, breathing to release stress, taking a walk, etc.—to remove the barriers in our lives and set up daily routines and traditional practices, we can identify and connect with supports that help us achieve our full potential and improve our quality of life.

Consider this: In life, there is a healing stream that is built to strengthen us and connect us to an ongoing flow. Setting up AM is that healing stream that takes us out of a negative vibration of hate, fear, and feeling of less than, and of creating a vortex of negativity. AM starts with reimagining a better way of experiencing, walking through, and simply being in the world.

As you may have witnessed or experienced, many people are stuck—unable to see any bright periods or best days. Sometimes our thinking becomes altered, confused, overwhelmed, and disorganized, resulting in feelings of being shattered. Yet, we carry and hold on to the broken pieces, which are a spirit of heaviness and defeat, and we are unable to find the path toward peace and serenity.

Defining and creating better moments can help us become aware and increase our wisdom, knowledge, and truth. What is the meaning of life, and how can the broken pieces be used to build better moments? In life, there are situations and problems fueled by choices and stressful situations that cause a loop of repetitive and destructive broken cycles. Imagine people's eyes are open, but their eyes are working as if they are closed, blocking them from seeing beauty, joy, and possibility, and from living their best moments.

If you are stuck in a period of waiting, it is time for what I call Alabaster Moments. I use AM as a metaphor for the coming together of alabaster, a precious moldable gem, and moments in time to help move from being stuck to using your situation for transformation. As we look to understand and gain knowledge, we begin to open our awareness so we can commit to better situations and times in life. Defining moments in life give a positive viewpoint and create a space for continued growth and empowerment. These moments become an activation to further jump-start and help support a better and new awareness, feeling, and experience.

Are you in need of a fresh, new, transformational restart in life? It is time to focus and think of new ways to innovate your life by taking the broken pieces and creating a mosaic; a beautiful abstract painting; a masterpiece; or a map for life from the fragments of disjointed pain, heated situations, pressures, and painful memories. If you are in a place of pause and inactivity because pain, hurt, and suffering have consumed your moments, or a place of pause in which your life is on hold, begin to see with the eyes of the Spirit every good and perfect gift. Use those broken pieces to make that beautiful work of art, and use your experiences to live a better, fulfilling life.

The voice of the Spirit has been speaking to me for years to bring Alabaster Moments to the world. The other voice—the negative one— has kept repeating that nobody wants to know about Alabaster Moments. It tells me that AM is too simple to even talk about; of course, people know they should be having good moments.

But the inner whisper continued to give me guidance and understanding, and I realized we have the power to shape and mold our life. We have the gift of decision-making to create moments that heal, empower, and help us to build upon and grow.

I have been supplying services in the healing arts for many years. I continue to see individuals stuck, perhaps because of life choices, failing to move forward, or constantly repeating all the bad things that have happened in their life. Their message to the world is that they have no goodness and life has not been good to them. Their lens is closed, and the bad habits and choices continue to dominate their life moments. They have aligned with that which is not good, and it has become a part of their identity and life story. They are not holding on or thinking of any safe, peaceful places and cannot imagine the good things. All of their narratives are negative, and they focus on encounters that have disempowered them. What I am proposing is to create new memories to build a better and continuously solid foundation to return and recreate more goodness. To understand that when we feel sad, that can lead to secondary feelings such as worthlessness. To develop ways to feel better and to develop this foundation as a place to return.

We do not have to be in a period of waiting for things to get better and have good points. My mind, will, and emotions are connected and fixed to this calling. It is a call that I must answer to help encourage myself and others to live better intentional moments, and to hold on to empowering moments in time. It is at the center and innermost part of my thinking to approach life by building great experiences that support self-confidence, self-esteem, positivity, and ongoing well-being. So many moments can shape us in life, and sometimes we get stuck in the mold, never to show our significance, beauty, impact, and gifts to the world. A renewing of the mind, body, spirit, and heart from the inside out can build a transformative life by creating good, positive practices and experiences.

AM is about remembering joyful moments that make you feel speechless and alive. It is important to understand that when dealing with feelings and states of being that include; anxiety, grief and bereavement, mood swings, depression, anger, resentment, frustration, sadness, loss, confusion, agitation, panic, high-energy states, creativity, love, loneliness, boredom, emptiness, obsessiveness, heartbreak, and general emotional pain, we can focus and decide to elevate ourselves to have better times.

When we connect to meaning and purpose in life, we are guided to a better flow of happiness, fulfillment, and good relationships. AM helps us to stay aligned to our life force and operate within our full potential. When we realize our potential, we mold our aspirations to aid in shaping our contribution to the world and the next generation. Living with ongoing stressful feelings and emotions leads to tension, and difficulty growing and deepening our experiences. The mind is one of the most powerful things, but the mind can misfire and be rigid, stopping the flow of right thinking that leads to happiness. In life, we can be in a place of being unable to be productive or see anything good. We can also be stuck in bad flashes of time. When we are in a state of flowing, we can be compared to water. Water always finds its way around the biggest mountain.

Remember:

- In life, we must find our way around wrong things and choices.
- We must get to a place where we are living as part of our higher self.
- Be intentional; speak positively of yourself and your life.
- Use kind words to yourself and others.
- Focus and highlight the positive experiences.
- Focus on small victories.
- Find ways and times to encourage yourself.
- Speak from a place of power and truth.

Chapter 1

A LETTER TO GOD

I have been on a spiritual path since my childhood, attending church with my grandmother, Mama Honey. My grandmother was an usher in the church. She wanted to serve more but was fearful because she could not read or write. I would watch her filled with fear, afraid she would be called upon to read.

She could not read or write but she was courageous and a strong woman of prayer and faith.

For the larger part, it was my experiences at the church that has made me so very intrigued by spirituality and the continuous reviving of the spirit. I will share a letter I wrote to God while attending a Beautiful Warrior class—a Bible study class that was offered by the church. In the letter, I stated that I wanted to be like the alabaster woman who gave God the highest honor by pouring out love, peace, joy, suffering, gentleness, goodness, faith, meekness, and temperance. Even back then, the message of Alabaster Moments was in my heart. I have held on to this letter since the year 2010. It is copied over from my handwritten records and reads:

A Letter from Sharon Jones on February 16, 2010, to GOD

First of all, dear God, I am grateful for my journey thus far. Over the past years, I have started to evolve even more in understanding that I am an extension of source energy. I am a creator and the thoughts of the mind, and the spoken words give me your power. I have seen a lot of powerful energy from others that have brought me great experiences in my life. I take the positive pictures seen in life to create and build more life. So, I continue to sojourn here on earth and my desire is to develop more positive inner strength to further tap into the power of God to recognize the ability to call those things that are not like they were. Enhancing my strength and courage to empower others with the knowledge and truth of God, to walk in victory, abundance, and receive all of their dreams and divine destiny connecting heaven to earth under an open heaven. I ask God for new revelations each day and ways to apply these revelations to my life in areas of relationships, wisdom, finances, health, and perfect self-expression. To be like the alabaster woman giving God the highest honor by pouring out love, peace, joy, long-suffering, gentleness good-ness, faith, meekness, and temperance. I would like to connect so much with the source to find myself in a place, called there like Elijah where the Ravens will feed me by the brook. That all famines are over in my life, whether physical, spiritual, or mental, and my steps are being ordered by the Lord and I am plugged into his power, wisdom, peace, and love. I want my latter to be greater, connected and listening with the ears of the spirit, seeing with the eyes of the spirit, touching others with the spirit, hearing and understanding the wisdom of the spirit, and always tasting and seeing that the Lord is good, and His mercies endure forever, so my heart's desire is to have a peaceful home, a wonderful soul mate chosen by God, financial abundance, an overflow, perfect health, explosive wisdom and knowledge, and a life of bliss and harmonic wealth totally aligned with God source. For I believe that we are here to bless and prosper others and my goal is to reflect this belief in my daily interactions. I accept divine guidance and I feel safe, secure, hopeful, and protected by divine love. Asking God to bless me indeed, enlarge my territory, and keep his hand with me that I may not cause pain but be a shining light, helping others to get their breakthroughs and walk in their divine destiny, connected 100% to Christ and fully aligned with God.

Chapter 2

MESSAGE FROM YOURSELF IN THE MAIL

"Your task is not to seek for love, but merely to seek and find all the barriers within yourself that you have built against it."

– Rumi

Messages come to us in many ways and forms: in dreams, through prayer, while listening to music, through the Spirit, and through circumstances. Imagine that you receive a letter in the mail that is filled with all of your negative thoughts, beliefs, and self-talk. The letter includes the following messages:

- You have not done anything in life
- You cannot relax
- Your mind is troubled
- You do not have enough money
- No one will help you
- You cannot do anything for yourself
- You should be further in life
- You do not have any energy to move forward
- You cannot see the good
- You should be living better
- You have experienced many heavy situations in life

- You have made many mistakes
- You have become stuck
- You are weighed down by circumstances
- You do not have any joy
- You have made many mistakes
- You are buried beneath the goodness in your life
- You have suppressed the good
- You will need to reestablish Alabaster Moments

The solution that I am proposing is to begin where you are right now and get comfortable with the mindset that you deserve to have good, that you can live and experience better moments in your life. If we reflect back and focus on even the tiniest, simple circumstances, we can spark life. All it takes is a tiny spark to ignite a fire. By taking intentional action, by recognizing and holding moments in time as sacred, we begin to live with more alertness, freedom, and life.

What messages do you really hold on to and fully believe? Are the messages you tell yourself serving your good and supporting your life purpose? It is time to start seeing what messages we are holding firmly to, embracing the meaning of the messages we tell ourselves, and sending them out to others and the world.

Another thing is where the messages are coming from and how healthy the people and places that you have received the messages from are. Did you receive them from a trusted messenger that can bring meaningful information and positive change?

Imagine beginning a process of using intentional moments for transformation and receiving another letter in the mail with the following messages:

- You have done everything right in your life
- You relax so easily and effortlessly
- Your mind is so at ease

- You are overflowing with abundance
- You are supported by many people
- You take care of yourself with healing hands
- You take the initiative to help yourself
- You are just where the divine wants you in life
- Your energy is restored each day
- You see the good everywhere
- You are living vibrantly
- The situations you have experienced in life are light as a feather
- You have learned many powerful lessons
- You are flowing like the water
- You recognize that your circumstances were anchoring you down, causing you to be stuck and unable to move to a better place
- Your joy is restored
- Your mistakes are now monuments of greatness
- You are on top, with the goodness in your life
- You arise in life with great goodness
- Your goodness is radiated to all

Moments play a significant role in our life. Regardless of what we are going through, we can still have good times and special moments. We also have the free will to choose our moments, of which there are many, and to make meaning out of them.

Chapter 3

DEFINITION OF ALABASTER MOMENTS

Alabaster is a precious mineral that can be carved and shaped. When light is placed within the carving, its beauty is magnified. It is formed under high temperatures and pressure to become metamorphic rocks and is often used to build a base for sculptures. Alabaster is known to symbolize purity, virtue, and transparency; the whiter the stone, the better. It encourages feelings of peace and calmness and can help to combat stress, heal arguments, or calm anger in the household. It is a protective stone, especially for babies, children, and anyone innocent at heart. Alabaster also has purifying and cleansing properties. As such, it is important and beneficial to use a vessel made of alabaster to hold loose herbs or a cleansing stick for use in your smoke-cleansing practice.

What is a Moment?

A moment is a brief period of time. Moments include watching the powerful ocean, beautiful green lush forests, tall strong mountains, forceful waterfalls, and beautiful colorful flower gardens.

Some moments derail and disorganize the balance and harmony in our lives. When we connect the meaning and properties of alabaster to the meaning of moments, we see the unique extraordinary moments that bring us amazement and enrich our lives so much that we have to pinch ourselves to see if things are real. Sometimes, our brokenness is shaped by moments of losing a loved one, job, relationship, or housing, deteriorating health, and many other life events and situations.

Alabaster Moments

Alabaster Moments is a philosophy of positive change, a sacred walk, a powerful focus that calls out the very best within you. It is about returning to the sacred to heal and transform lives.

It is the spontaneous, natural occurrence of, or setting up of an experience in which, through your actions or someone else's actions, your life is changed in a positive way forever. Each time you think and reflect on that place/moment in time, it becomes a spark that ignites your life; your happiness is restored, your spirit is renewed, and you look forward to the experience again. The concept of Alabaster Moments was formed from the divine inspiration of the Spirit. Alabaster is a mineral, and one of its uses is to hold rare, valuable, and expensive oils and perfumes.

You are alabaster and you can recreate those rare, valuable, and sustainable moments. The many experiences that occur in our lives and the messages that we attach to those experiences sometimes need to be reshaped to bring the fragrance back into our lives. We must construct moments in life for a renewal of mind, body, and Spirit in an environment that supports an abundant and radiant life. By forming Alabaster Moments in your life, you restore the powerful spirit within, leading to an alignment of the mental, physical, spiritual, and emotional, and restoring joy and hope.

Encounters of Restoration

AM consists of encounters in which your life is restored, shaped, and changed forever in a positive way. Think about the positive moments that give you strength, courage, and the will to keep going and living life. Moments are a powerful catalyst to help radiate happiness, restoration, and the renewal of your mind, body, and spirit. These important encounters help us to walk through life more empowered and give us powerful memories.

Majestic Rising

Alabaster Moments consists, too, of the majestic rising of self. You find comfort where all is well, your thoughts are positive, and you are relaxed and content, enjoying life to the fullest. You are in alignment. All fear is gone, you are hopeful for tomorrow, you feel powerful and courageous, and you do not want the moment to ever end. You are one with the divine Creator, God.

Utopia

The message of Alabaster Moments is about creating magnificent moments of utopia. Have you ever gone to a place where all is balanced and harmonious? Where there is a flow like water, nothing is getting in the way of anything, you do not want to leave, and you want to return to that perfect place again mentally and physically? It is a safe, beautiful place.

Alabaster Moments can be compared to utopia. In the Holy Scriptures, the Garden of Eden is described as a utopia. The beautiful garden contained the tree of life and is where God intended Adam and Eve to live in peaceful and contented innocence, effortlessly reaping the beautiful gifts and fruits of the earth. It was a place of perfection where everything was perfect, good, safe, and secure, and all needs were provided easily and effortlessly.

Words and phrases that describe Alabaster Moments:

Utopia—a place of ideal perfection

Arcadia—a region or scene of simple pleasure and quiet   Dreamland—an unreal delightful country existing only in imagination or in dreams

Dreamworld—a world of illusion or fantasy

Fairyland— a place of delicate beauty or magical charm

Wonderland—a place that excites admiration or wonder

Blessedness—having a sacred nature: connected with God; very welcome, pleasant, or appreciated

bliss— complete happiness

blissfulness—full of, marked by or causing complete happiness

Euphoria—a feeling of well-being or elation, gladness; experiencing pleasure, joy, or delight

joy—a feeling of great happiness

Shangri-la—a remote beautiful imaginary place where life approaches perfection

Ariba—The seventh heaven, which borrows some concepts from its Jewish counterpart, is depicted as being composed of divine light incomprehensible to the mortal man.

Garden of Eden—The beautiful garden which had the tree of life, and the place God intended Adam and Eve to live in peaceful and contented innocence, effortlessly reaping the fruits of the Earth. The garden also held the tree of knowledge and of good and evil, from which Adam and Eve were forbidden to eat.

Eden—the symbolic space of perfect harmony, the place in which absolute happiness reigns. It is nothing less than what is guessed to have been; that which God imagined as the zenith of creation and paradise. But humanity has sought it on Earth as if it were a secret garden.

Promised Land (in the Bible)—the land of Canaan, which was promised to Abraham and his descendants (Gen. 12:7). A place or situation in which someone expects to find great happiness.

Chapter 4

WEARY ON THE JOURNEY

When we face many situations and happenings in our lives, we can become weakened and lose awareness of and sight in life. We may be strong, but the load may be too much for us to carry, and we may not have the awareness or the energy to carry it. So, we try to keep walking but the baggage we are carrying and holding on to is weighing us down. We become overburdened and forget that we are also carrying beautiful gifts that have become hidden away from view.

Have you ever thought about how you are walking throughout your daily life? The Bible encourages us to walk by faith and not by sight, and to walk by the spirit of God, who is the light. Many of us walk through life easily distracted and unable to focus on making positive changes. Let us instead reflect on our actions and walk with awareness and focus to free our mind, body, and spirit of the negativity weighing us down.

Lao Tzu says 'the journey of a thousand miles starts with the first step.' We have to start somewhere to reach our destination, a place of really living life. Alabaster Moments is about stepping into a new day and a new way to think of and create goodness. When we realize that we have these precious gifts we can focus and tap into them to fire up our energy to keep walking the path. During this walk, we begin to tap into that precious energy that helps us to keep walking to reach our destination. And we may travel many paths that lead to multiple destinations.

Sometimes it feels like we are walking through the fire, but we are not burned. Our intuition sets in, and wisdom comes forth. This positive wisdom begins the process of alignment in our life.

Albert Einstein said that imagination is more powerful than knowledge. So, let us imagine the heavy bags falling, dropping, and releasing from our lives—the bags of sadness, grief, loss, hopelessness, anxiety, lack, hate, unforgiveness, shame, blame, abuse, and interrupted dreams. Think about the negative things you are holding on to in your mind, body, spirit, and environment, and as you walk, use your imagination to drop those bags so that you can begin to think of the positive within and around you.

Many people aspire to live out their purpose on earth while some just stumble purposeless; they do not listen to the small whisper of God, whether in the mind or through universal signs, which supplies guidance and instructions.

The small whisper has given instructions to people to author books, start blogs or podcasts, become teachers, spiritual healers, motivators, or pioneers. The small voice has given many a major message to deliver themselves to the world in a way that would change it and the lives of others.

Yet, many are so overwhelmed with life they are literally stuck. They have ears but are unable to hear. They have a heart but are unable to feel. They have a mind but are unable to think the right thoughts. They have so many great ideas, gifts, and talents and yet, they cannot move forward; they cannot make room to utilize their gifts. They are full yet empty and stuck in a moment of time in which they cannot do anything. They are not living to their full capability. They are sad and overwhelmed, with too much chaos within them, and they are in need of guidance.

Alabaster Moments is about the turnaround from negativity to positivity. It is about positive moments beginning to flow in our lives and it is when we experience a clear shift toward the positive seeds that have been planted within us that are beginning to grow. With AM, we can begin to fertilize, water, and cultivate them. It is important to turn our focus from weariness to rejuvenation, freshness, and liveliness, and to decide to get up and live in wellness. As part of our journey in life, sometimes we feel we do not have the energy, strength, or time to complete tasks and keep things moving in a positive way. We start to align with negative words, beliefs, and experiences that we hear from ourselves and others and we begin to lose our strength. The negative words that we hear, coupled with our negative experiences, can hinder our positive flow in life. We start to question where we are in life, start to feel alone, friendless, disappointed, and not in a good place. Most people journey through life filled with hesitation, interruptions, and distractions and remain consumed with all the bad memories they have faced in life—a heavy load that only seems to grow more difficult to carry.

I am fortunate to have grown up with a focus to honor what the Spirit is saying and revealing to me, and to have grown up knowing the power of the Holy Spirit.

Life is such a mystery; we have no memories prior to our birth. We come into the world as a blank, clean canvas. We can use that canvas to paint all bad circumstances or situations, or we can paint those things that give us life, contribute to our life force and energy, and radiate goodness, beauty, peaceful energy, and joy. Living and walking in the Spirit, being aligned with him, helps us to keep a vision of love, hope, and forgiveness, and gives us confidence that good things are happening.

Sometimes we find ourselves in a place of trouble where the waters are raging and turbulence is all around us. When in such situations, the gift of resilience is produced and becomes an anchor. Embracing these situations helps us cleanse and build our resilience. When we are in a low place, we can build ourselves up in ways, such as listening to music or talking to a supportive friend. We need to seek a higher vibration and take action to affirm positive intentions, speaking blessings over our lives, opening our hearts and filling it with gratitude in order to rise to that level and draw positive experiences to us.

God can also fill us up when we are empty; He is full of glory and has marvelous power. When watching the waves of the ocean, for example, I see the massive power of our Creator. As I watch the water flow around the rocks, my soul is soothed, and I can imagine my life easily flowing. I often read and imagine the stories in the holy sacred book as well, and I wonder, as I hope you do: What if we came into the world proclaiming our blessings and being intentional about focusing on good moments? What if our first lesson and moment of understanding was the blessing of gratitude, and a reminder to see the good, bright moments in life?

In life, we can be focused on all the things that have failed our expectations, disappointed us, and blocked our pathways. We often turn our back on good and positive events. Our path is often a destructive one, and we focus on all the hurts and setbacks, pouring out tons and tons of negative energy. When the sudden happens, it gets us off the path of belief and interrupts our faith. Faith is confidence in God and releasing our cares to Him so that we do not have to carry that weight. Many times, we say that we have released our cares yet we keep worrying and talking about our problems, releasing more of that negative energy. As a result, we begin to feel depleted of our life force. As such, it is important to live out your moments fully and with intention, not just go along off fumes. These fumes will not carry us very far unless they are sparked by a person or situation. The positive actions of others may ignite our fumes and renew us, helping us to feel encouragement, hope, confidence, and more.

My faith led me to undergo the biggest journey in my life: traveling from a small town in the deep South to the large city of San Francisco on the bus with only a handful of change. I did not know what to expect but I was looking for a brighter way to help myself and my family. I held tightly to that change—a valuable gift that was given to me by my father. It was not much but he gave me all he had.

I traveled from bus station to bus station and only got off the bus when necessary. On my journey, I met very nice, caring people who shared their food and substance with me. I held close to my faith and arrived in San Francisco safely.

My bus ride to California has become one of my Alabaster Moments. The handful of change was the catalyst for new beginnings and positive change. This journey was a point in time that shaped and molded my life. Of course, there is more to the story that I may share one day, but the important thing to note is that this brief period of time changed my life.

AM sparks life and builds up our strength and resiliency. When we are making meaning out of life we must:

SEEK

See with the eyes of the Spirit

Enter a mindset of more than enough

Enter a relationship with God

Keep God's word close to our hearts

Chapter 5

BROKEN VESSELS

In the Holy Scriptures, a vessel is described as a person who has been selected and chosen by God to do great things. A broken vessel is a person who is destroyed or forgotten, or who feels flawed or broken. I see myself as a chosen vessel to do magnificent work in the name of God, our Creator.

In life, we receive many messages. Some make us feel good and empowered and others make us feel that we will never meet the bar because it is too high. When the latter happens, it may cause us to constantly think about how things are not going the way that they should or happening the way we think they should. We can be compared to a broken vessel, carrying a substance that does not have meaning or produce a great fragrance in life, just like the woman who broke the alabaster box. The vessel has holes that sometimes release anger, hurt, sadness, and only minimal glimmers of joy and happiness.

Furthermore, we are living in an age where we want things to come fast and receive them right away without any preparation or purposefulness. In today's culture exists a lack of gratitude and a focus on entitlement. Thus, we interrupt our Alabaster Moments through our inability to appreciate these wonderful moments.

AM is about purposely focusing on and setting up great moments to heal and repair these holes. The messages that we accept as our truth can either empower us or make us tired and distort our view of reality. In most cases, situations derail us so easily that we become lethargic and defeated very quickly. They can consume our entire blueprint for life and cause us to be unable to cope in a positive manner, change, and release the fragrance in our lives. Too often, we seem to pour out the not-so-good and set up a cycle of the ongoing negative release of our problems, always craving the good but not doing anything to obtain it. We continue to release these negative conversations throughout our lives. Instead, we must fill ourselves with a beautiful fragrance to create a helpful, healing transformative part of ourselves. When we breathe in and release peacefulness and good thoughts, we are pouring out and designing Alabaster Moments (AM), which are powerful, sustainable moments that bring reminders of relief and better days.

Shaping Broken Pieces

When we are broken, we can take the broken pieces to create and mold our lives to significance. Our life can become a shining masterpiece. As a practitioner of the healing arts, I continue to build a transformational, sacred approach to connecting the concepts of Alabaster Moments and delivering life-changing solutions and strategies for spiritual renewal for individuals feeling overwhelmed, counted out, less than, messed up, and tangled up.

I use my calling to the world and my mantra of Alabaster Moments to facilitate a process of life growth, healing, and transformation. As we align with our life purpose, we also align with all our positive flow and life force, which we can use to mold and secure our lives with greatness, pressing beyond painful memories. It is my experience and belief that reflecting on amazing moments can cause the restoration of our lives.

Sometimes, we feel counted out and uncertain, not knowing where to turn or what to do. We are in search of meaning that can lead to healing and hope. And so, we are at a point in which there is a need for a spiritual transformation—believing in something greater than ourselves. Our uncertainty causes a shift in our mind, body, and spirit, which become unaligned. When we are out of alignment, our thinking is altered and we are unable to have the right thoughts. Fear begins to set in and it is difficult to have faith or to know that something good is going to happen;

we then have difficulty engaging in self-care. Fear can be numbing and devastating and cause us to become indecisive or unwilling to act. This builds up and can cause an increase in anxiety and depression. The cause of the fear can center around many themes and situations, all of which interrupt our good moments. When this happens, we can seek a spiritual transformation, which is a noticeable change in a person's sacred or spiritual life.

One way to get out of this negative thinking and cycle is through gratitude, a catalyst for receiving more goodness in life. When we are intentional about practicing gratitude, we begin to come alive and feel immense joy and renewal. One way to keep gratitude at the forefront is to build a life of special moments consistently. Take note of the moments that bring you peace and happiness. Reflect upon those moments and think of them with gratitude, especially when you are feeling down.

Release the Baggage

In life, we can be focused on all the things that have failed our expectations, disappointed us, and blocked our pathways. We often turn our back on the good and highlight everything that we do not like that does not serve us. Our way is often a destructive path filled with broken cycles, and we replay them and focus on all the hurts and setbacks, pouring out tons and tons of wasted energy.

This derails us from the path of believing and interrupts our faith. When we become overwhelmed, our faith can begin to grow dim. Faith changes the seasons of our life. The more faith we have, the more miracles we receive. The most valuable moments in life grow and feed our faith, and faith is strengthened by giving to others.

There is power in changing the flow of our energy to something positive. Imagine what would happen if we changed our focus, trusted the process, and expected positive results. What if we begin to look for the positive in every situation?

The beginning of releasing baggage is to practice being still, acknowledging our feelings, and sitting in silence to clear and renew our minds. Releasing baggage helps us to work through our difficult relationships and traumatic encounters, and to be able to observe patterns and opportunities to heal and transform. It is important to be honest with yourself, practice patience, and to understand that it requires commitment to work on your recovery plan. Do not hold on to unhealthy toxic emotions—that is baggage. This includes any unresolved emotional confusion caused by a variety of experiences, such as childhood trauma, abuse, or any negative experience from the past. It is important to be intentional about living from a place of positivity and reaching for a positive approach.

Feelings of Inadequacy and Shame

In life, sometimes we see ourselves as less than others. We can start to describe ourselves as losers and start to persecute ourselves with negative words. We begin to view our lives as inadequate and incomplete. We think that we are disappointments and ineffective in all that we do. We begin to align with negative feelings, becoming let down, and setting ourselves back.

This is where the power of Alabaster Moments comes in. The broken pieces of our identity are used to rebuild, reposition, reassess, rethink, reconstruct, restructure, and revolutionize our life.

Learning How to Have Brighter Moments

Creating brighter moments helps us to see a new narrative emerge in our lives. There is a shift when we look for good things. When we shift to looking for and expecting good, we can see hope and possibility.

We can create an environment for restoration to help navigate and emerge from life's challenges with renewed optimism. We can create and set aside time for an ongoing routine to treat ourselves well and honor ourselves, as well as identifying and surrounding ourselves with loving and supportive family and friends. Bright moments come when we develop a spiritual practice or daily routine that is filled with gratitude.

What I have seen is that a book is a wonderful tool to awaken a person and help them to release their potential and restore their greatness. A book can take them places that they may never be able to go or experience. Books are so beneficial because they stir up the imagination. If we can imagine it, we can believe it and achieve it.

In my opinion, a book is the greatest gift you can give someone because its content is poured from one's soul, within their spirit; it ignites intelligence and passion. The philosophy of AM is about seeing moments in life as a gift, and in a book, you can relive the moments poured out of the soul of others—also a gift— to strengthen you. For example, you can learn about AM and want to live more of these bright moments.

So, if you feel there is too much chaos in your life, it is time to reduce the chaos by building up positive moments and stories to restore your life. So, we must be focused on releasing the energy of chaos. State your intention through the following mantra:

The altar is a place of prayer, worship, release, renewal, and new beginnings. I will lay all the broken negative pieces down at the altar. As I lay the broken pieces down, I spiritually transform them. The broken pieces that will be laid down are:

Hopelessness	Helplessness	Pain	Suffering
Chaos	Wrong thinking	Negative thoughts	Defeat
Drama	Negative self-talk	Shame	Guilt
Depression	Failure	Anxiety	Loss
Hurt	Fear	Grief	Disappointment
Lack of self-love	Panic	Sleepless nights	Lack of self-worth
Weak faith	Trouble	Lack	Scarcity

Hope	Helpful	Healing	Happiness
Peace	Right Thinking	Positive Thoughts	Victory
Powerful Stories	Positive Self-Talk	Grace	Innocence
Cheerfulness	Success	Calmness	Recovery
Sufficiency	Confidence	Joy	Overflow Of Love And Joy
Abundance Of Self-Love	Relaxation	Sleep	Order
Strong Faith			

The broken pieces are turned into Alabaster Moments of:

A-L-A-B-A-S-T-E-R

- Appreciation
- Learning experience
- An "aha" moment
- Having a brilliant idea
- Awakening
- Sensibility
- Timely thought
- Epiphany
- Enlightenment
- Eye-opening
- Realization
- Revelation

Chapter 6

SETTING YOURSELF FREE THROUGH PRAYER

Alabaster Moments is about being an external manifestation of positive energy, promoting perseverance, strength, resiliency, and hope. It is about being able to improve and change the fragrance of your life and the lives of others through empowerment, genuine care, concern, commitment, and spiritual enlightenment.

In 2004, I attended a woman's conference in Berkeley, CA. There, twenty women wore chains around their necks and carried heavy bags filled with rocks and hurtful words that had put them down throughout their journey.

The highlight of the conference was the prayer to set yourself free. It began with honoring the name of Jesus. It called for the binding of mind, body, and spirit to the purpose and will of God, our Creator. It called for the spirit of truth, awareness of self, and the power of the blood of Jesus. It encouraged us to take notice of our powerful Creator and how He works in our life each and every day.

The prayer called for aligning our minds—our thoughts, purposes, and feelings—to the mind of Christ. It called for binding our feet to the path God has ordained us to walk, to strengthen our steps to be strong and steady. It focused on the work of the cross, which is about God's mercy, truth, love, power, forgiveness, and humility.

It introduced the loosening of what is referred to as the strong man—

he who binds us to our negative situations and takes our power away from us—and his hold on everything he had ever stolen. It introduced the rebuking of words and loosening the power of every moment of deception and negative influence against us.

The prayer called for the repentance of having wrong attitudes and thoughts. It included asking for forgiveness of self and others. It called forth tearing down and destroying every negative hold that has been constructed in our lives that we continue to hold on to. It called on us to focus on our attitudes and patterns and overcome the negative, non-beneficial behaviors. It called out our spiritual desires that line up with receiving the fruit of the Holy Spirit. It called for the loosening of the strangleholds in life, and any wrong feelings that we may have against anyone. It called for us to remember to forgive others who have caused us pain, loss, or grief, and to be mindful of the power and the effects of any harsh words spoken by ourselves or others.

I believe strongly in the power of reading and speaking prayers. I have held on to this Cherokee prayer for over twenty years. It is one of my Alabaster Moments.

The Lord's Prayer in Cherokee

Our Father, Heaven dweller
My loving will be to thy name
Your Lordship, let it make its appearance
Here on Earth—let happen what you think
The same as in Heaven is done
Daily our food, give to us this day
Forgive us our debts, the same as we forgive our debtors
And do not temptation being lead us into
Deliver us from evil existing
For thine, your Lordship is
And the glory is forever
AMEN

Chapter 7

PLACE OF WAITING

Encounters of being courageous are fully documented in the holy sacred Scriptures. These encounters really speak to my heart and stir up my will to keep going. There have been times in my life when I have felt inadequate, like the underdog, made fun of, mistreated, excluded, and seen as less than others. And I know there are others who have felt and still feel the same way. After all, I have supplied service to others for many years, many of whom are in a place or period of waiting for transformation and positivity. They have fully aligned with and embraced the negative messages spoken by others. They ignore good things that bring joy and regard benefits as non-important. Everything is reversed, as they become comfortable in their negative state, finding it safe and familiar. There has been a deceptive switch away from the sacred and there is no divine anchor or guidance. Their lives are missing the divine truth that promotes life and sacred blessings.

Being connected to the divine increases life force energy and helps us to stay positive and not drift away. When we are disconnected from our divine creator, it is like a power cord disconnected from an electric current. We become powerless and feeble. As such, we keep trying to get better and stronger, but without the right connection.

Are you in a place of pause, waiting to live again, but cannot activate your purpose and passion? Review your life to see what the areas of pause are that are interrupting you from living fully.

Do you keep thinking over and over that you will get to it—to thinking positively, living life fully—eventually? When reality and actions are overpowered because so many things are going on, those important moments can be placed on hold. The zest for life needs to be resuscitated with a new walk and new talk so that you may breathe freely and easily.

The reality is that we have to open up to wonderful times and be intentional about seeing the sparkle that life offers and maintaining that shine. For example, visualize a fire that is flickering. Imagine the flames are trying to ignite but need that special moment or experience to fan them. Do not allow the flames to flicker and be blown by the wind; do not let them go out.

Throughout my experience supplying care in a therapeutic setting, I have realized that many are in a continuous period or phase of busyness: they pile on too many things at once and are unable to manage them well, which causes uncertainty. Their energy is wasted on efforts that do not bring about positive or meaningful impact or fruits of their labor. They think they are moving, but really, they are stuck digging a horrible pit that they cannot climb out of. It is difficult for them to move forward and feel prosperous in life.

I am encouraging you to start right now to set up times and create special moments that make you feel and come alive. It is time to focus on creating better life sparks—Alabaster Moments.

Remember, too, that the Bible speaks about becoming brand new! Here are some things that create a spark/turning point in life:

- Renewed spirit
- Miracles
- New learning
- Restorative life situations
- Renewed mind
- Caring for others
- Believing by faith
- Honoring ourselves
- Receiving God's favor
- Loving ourselves

Chapter 8

THE NEED FOR RESUSCITATION

"At times, our own light goes out and is rekindled by a spark from another person. Each of us has cause to think with deep gratitude of those who have lighted the flame within us."

– Albert Schweitzer

I have witnessed and learned that it is not beneficial to align with thoughts that do not produce better feelings. It seems more and more people do not feel their best. Their mind is confused, inundated with concerns, disorganized, broken, and they feel defeated in so many ways. As such, they are going about their life viewing themselves in a distorted way. Rather than using their broken pieces to make something beautiful, they are simply trying to hold on to the pieces and continuing the negative cycle. They need a jumpstart to help support a new awareness, feeling, and experience. They need a fresh new transformational restart in their life.

I have noticed, too, that many are not conducting themselves in ways that bring about meaningful or healthy moments that move their life forward, toward greatness or productivity. It is like being in a storm with high winds all the time, unable to find a peaceful place. The disorganization and turmoil rob us of our purpose and passion in life. The destructive cycle of painful thoughts, memories, and mental models cancel out sacred moments of healing and being.

Many people need new ways to innovate their life. Their fire and flames, meaning and purpose need to be returned and their zest for life needs to be resuscitated to usher in a new perspective. As I mentioned in the introduction, one way of doing so is by taking the fragments of pain and negativity and creating a masterpiece.

In spite of our painful memories, we have the power to bounce back. This power is called personal resiliency. We become stronger, able to manage stress, and function better when faced with challenges, adversity, and trauma. Resilience brings hope, optimism, and self-confidence. It helps us to solve problems, take care of ourselves, and ask for help. Personal resiliency is cultivated by taking care of ourselves and managing our emotions.

Resiliency starts in the mind. We have the emotional mind, which is filled with passion, love, nurture, and excitement. But despair and nervousness are also experienced in this state of mind at high levels of intensity. Within the emotional mind, facts can be skewed because people will act based on feelings.

The reasonable mind, however, is based on rules, logic, facts, and data. The wise mind is the integration of the emotional and reasonable mind. Operating in the wise mind helps us to make decisions that are effective. We should not let anything interfere with setting up the nurturing of our spirit. We can nurture and choose to develop protective factors to support our life.

Several protective factors that I use in my life are:

- Believing that it is OK to make mistakes in life
- Believing that it is OK to ask for help when it is needed
- A sense of self-efficacy
- A sense of personal control
- Positive spiritual beliefs

Chapter 9

USHERING IN THE RIGHT SPIRIT

John 4:24 – God is a Spirit: and they that worship him must worship him in spirit and in truth.

Ushering in the Spirit of Positivity

As a child, I learned early about the essence of God, the flowing of healing streams, and the transformational benefits—wisdom, focus, viewing myself in a better light— when the Spirit begins to move. I have been familiar with the power of God all my life. The Spirit is so important to living a wonderful, miraculous life. When we usher in the Spirit, we set up an environment for the Spirit to move. The environment must include:

- A silent and peaceful place free of disruptions
- Emptying and clearing your mind and heart from all alarms
- Reflecting and accepting forgiveness
- Engaging in uplifting moments of praise
- Aligning and listening for your spiritual truths
- Waiting patiently and allowing the Holy Spirit to move

Spiritual Transformation

A part of Southern tradition and spiritual transformation is to fast for two weeks and to pray as you are fasting. This is to build a relationship with God and get to know His spirit. Also included in this tradition is to acknowledge your belief in God and read the Bible, His spiritual truths. This ushers in closeness with the spirit of the living God. A part of this tradition includes baptism by water, which is an external show of your belief in God. To have this inside-out experience is a powerful renewing of the spirit.

Do not forget about embracing gratitude. Gratitude ushers in good and positive energy and the perfect environment for prosperity. When we replace the negative energy and usher in positive energy, we notice and highlight the positives in our lives. It is important to renew our spirit daily through gratitude, as this brings forth profound change.

Blessing Others Through Positive Words

May the words of my mouth and the meditations of my heart be acceptable in thy sight and bring healing, joy, blessings, benefit, comfort, contentment, ease, and favor to the world. May your spirit and positive energy be renewed each day with strength, new mercies, grace, power, love, gratitude, and spiritual fire and transformation throughout the earth. May bountiful blessings fill up your life spirit and familiarize you with ordinary happenings and daily occurrences minute by minute and second by second. May we align with our divine power and divine good to share with others and treat ourselves and others with kindness, compassion, and patience. May we speak blessings over others and use our words to elevate and transform.

Praise God from whom all blessings flow. This is the day that the Lord has chosen me as a vessel to welcome each of you to the center of my heart through Alabaster Moments. When we use kind words, it shows that we are ushering in a spirit of acceptance and love without judgment. It lets others know that we receive them openly with immense pleasure, hospitality, and an expression of sincere gratitude, all gift-wrapped in God's unconditional love. It encourages the serving of God and others in a spirit of truth, so the right spirit should be renewed daily. It ushers the spirit into, through the meditations of the heart, that which is good and positive. Affirm: I affirm through the power of devotion, using the gift of prayer. to always usher in and strive for kindness and to call everyone and every creature that has breath within them to be compassionate. For in God, our Creator, we live, move and have our being.

If joy is placed in everything outside of God, it can be lost in an instant. I ask that God bless me with His presence daily so that growth can take place and my expectations for positive moments of change will grow. When you crown your life with a bountiful harvest and give to others, even the most difficult of pathways overflow with abundance. Remember, joy does not come through your possessions but through your heart, which is the wellspring of life. A very powerful statement made by Dr. Martin Luther King is: "Everybody can be great because anybody can serve. You don't have to have a college degree to serve. You don't have to make your subject and verb agree to serve. You only need a heart full of grace."

Change in Perception

"There is nothing either good or bad but thinking makes it so."

– William Shakespeare

I used to let what I considered terrible, difficult, awful moments consume my life and make me feel inferior and hopeless. I would worry all the time and think about those difficult moments over and over. This would interfere with my mind, body, and spirit. So, I chose to decide which moments I would build that my life and foundation would center around. So, I am writing the dream that is flowing out of my heart and spirit that came as a small, recurrent whisper, that faint voice that you usually hear and ignore. I chose to not ignore that voice.

Vision

It is my vision and mission to create Alabaster Moments to transform lives so these moments can be passed on from generation to generation. I believe this can change the world. Alabaster Moments help you to come alive and feel immense joy, and building such powerful moments helps reset our lives. Begin to find your Alabaster Moments and build many more. Live from a place of creating great moments of freedom and healing. Restore and revive the spirit of self and others through positive inspiration, loving compassion, and effort. Think back to those wonderful moments that you want to relive.

We may be in a whirlwind of turbulence at times. We may not guard our gates—our physical senses—meaning our eyes, ears, mouth, and minds are filled with hopelessness. In other words, we are not aligning with that which is positive. Alabaster Moments is about redefining life to have better moments that lead to happiness, positivity, and ongoing renewal.

A   Allowing the positive to flow in your life

L   Loving your life to the fullest

A   Aligning with the Almighty

B   Believing by faith

A   Answering a negative with a positive

S   Streams of living water in the desert

T   Thinking about how you want your life to evolve

E   Entering into beautiful bliss through gratitude

R   Reaching out to others

The earth has been described by many people as a valley of sorrow. Somewhere along the way, there was shifting away from seeing, hearing, doing, and loving good. As we listen to the news, the broadcasts seldom relay something good. Bad news has become a billboard for the world.

But the holy sacred Scriptures say we should walk by faith and not by sight. Can you imagine that the very earth that we live on was spoken into existence by God? The place we refer to as earth was created to be a good place with all that we need. It was designed as a place filled with mountains, valleys, ridges, hills, peaks, and beautiful landscapes, with beautiful trees and flowers—a place designed to be where those made in the very image of God dwell. A place where we sometimes experience heavy burdens and feel down, weary, stressed, deficient, inferior, hateful, envious, and defeated.

Flowing from my heart is the message of AM, of being in a state of enjoyment, surrounded by good and powerful uplifting moments in life. To you, I send out the energy of healing, metamorphosis, and restoration.

Chapter 10

WHAT IS YOUR STORY?

Inspiration of the Spirit

"Sometimes reality is too complex. Stories give it form."

– Jean Luc Godard

Alabaster Moments comes out of inspiration from the Spirit, who guided me to bring and share to the world this concept. I think everyone can agree that the world needs more moments of healing. We can do this by choosing to love one another, forgiving one another, listening with our hearts, and seeing the good in others.

Just like the woman who broke the alabaster box and released the sweet perfume changed the fragrance of the room, we too can take the broken pieces, the moments that have broken us, and create harmony in our life, just like a beautiful mosaic or abstract painting to help to empower and transform ourselves and others.

What is your story?

How many people, if they were to take inventory and review their current lives as they see it today, could speak about feeling safe, secure, respected, living fully and experiencing great moments? What kind of lens are you looking through? A colorful lens, a narrow lens, a wide lens, a closed lens, or a lens of hate? How do you see your glass? As empty, half full, half empty, or refillable? Do you have a worldview that supports you and encourages you to love others? Remember that the spirit of love cultivates healing, connectedness, and forgiveness. Through this spirit, you will be able to develop that feeling of safety and live your life fully.

I mention earlier that AM is a sacred walk. When we return to the sacred, our steps and path are ordered by the divine. Everything you need, you will find on your pathway; it will be manifested. If you are seeing with the eyes of the spirit, you will become aware of when what you need and seek arrives. The help is within arm's reach if you open your eyes to see and your spirit to receive. When you are down and out, do not give up on hope; there is always a positive answer waiting. The Holy Scriptures say, "Let the weak say I am strong," and "Let your life shine." Look for moments that sparkle and exude positivity.

Point in Time

Are you someone who is overpowered by the feeling of being overwhelmed? Do you feel like you can never find time to focus, relax, enjoy the pleasures and goodness in life, and feel nourished and secure? Is it difficult for you to focus on life, not procrastinate, and bring things to completion? Do you feel that your life is rushed and that you do not have enough time to do things? That you are hopping from one thing to the next? Is it difficult for you to find your way?

Life can be very overwhelming sometimes, especially in today's age. Our minds tell us that we should always be busy and do multiple projects and multiple things to be productive. So, we continuously give ourselves task after task, and we end up getting caught up in circular—usually negative—energy and cannot seem to find our way or to find that place of comfort and serenity.

In most cases, we are barely holding on or functioning. Our energy levels are low, and our minds are racing, wandering, and unable to get to that place of harmony and balance, that place of peace and serenity in which we are really living life to the fullest and enjoying every moment. We are living in a time in which many people get up early in the morning and rush to get ready for the day, which is fast-paced and filled with chaos. Some work multiple jobs just to make a living, just trying to make it through the day to make it to that better life. They are not even aware of the beautiful moments in their life, as there are so many distractions that they forget to live life and really focus on the great moments that exist. Most are just barely hanging on and seemingly operating by default.

Now, factor in alabaster—a mineral that is easily molded—and moments—points in time. By using the metaphor of Alabaster Moments, you can mold your life to live vibrantly and fully free. You can savor the moments, see with the eyes of the Spirit, and find purpose, power, and potency in creating great moments. AM is being created so you can diminish and reduce the non-productive chaos that leads to stressful living.

You can deliver to yourself life-changing solutions and strategies for spiritual renewal through this proprietary transformative process of Alabaster Moments. AM will help you to enjoy life through the creation of positive moments, regardless of what is happening around you. It will help you build a story of transformation by renewing your belief to restore hope, action by action, by using the W.A.S. approach:

- Walk through it

- All is well (allow miracles to transpire)

- Seek a spiritual pathway to recovery

Chapter 11

EVERYDAY SACRED MOMENTS

We carry inside us the wonders we seek outside us.

– Rumi

Call to Really Start Living

Alabaster Moments are those experiences that you have positive memories of, and they continue to bring you joy, happiness, and fulfillment. The moment may begin when you are in a state of feeling hopeless and transform your circumstances into a life-changing experience. The moment is so clear in your mind that, no matter how much time has passed, it brings hope, an expectation of good, and a sense of care and security when you think of it.

Alabaster Moments may also be simple remembrances that bring you happiness. We can find AM in ordinary, day-to-day experiences and activities.

Remember your Alabaster Moments instead of talking about your negative moments and experiences. Alabaster Moments may include:

- Beautiful scenery such as a sunset or blue sky, the ocean, or a beautiful flower garden

- A neatly organized and decorated environment that is inspirational

- A surprise party

- A trip to Disney Land

- A trip to a beautiful resort

- A romantic dinner

- Receiving a beautiful gift

- Watching a motivational movie

- Hearing a powerful speech

- Reading an inspiring book

- Reconnecting with family

- A relaxing train ride

AM Means Being

AM is the occurrence or setting up of an experience that has a powerful outcome for your life. In the Holy Sacred Book, God responded to Moses, telling him "I AM THAT I AM." He was informing Moses of his existence, that he is real and alive. Reliving moments that are so powerful they render you speechless can make you feel alive and empower you to give with no limits, and to see little things as having a big impact.

My Alabaster Moments gave me the feeling of being alive while living in humble beginnings. Despite my humble way of living, I was in an environment of beautiful fruit-bearing trees, flowing rainwater in a barrel, soothing warmth from the fireplace, the smell of roasted sweet potatoes, a loving grandmother, mother, and father, and a brilliant brother.

I can recall wonderful walks with my grandmother to get wood for the fire, a flowing river that was beautiful and serene, and a path with trees on each side of the river. The holidays were made very special by my grandmother as she would create those very special boxes that I mentioned earlier.

I can recall, too, that wonderful pecan tree, which I called the giving-of-life tree, which helped sustain my family. Another moment was witnessing the bloom of the beautiful morning glory flowers in their majesty and beauty. There are so many memories that I am grateful to have shared with family, as well as just being in that beautiful area blessed by nature.

Also, when we lived in that area on Jim River, there were really intense thunderstorms and high winds, and I can remember my mother getting us ready to flee to the safety of our aunt's house, who lived down the road. I can remember the feeling of fear, uncertainty, and not knowing if our little house would withstand the storm. My family was really fearful of God's wrath, and chaos erupted during these storms. What I mean by this is that we felt that the house we were living in was not good enough to stay during a storm. But after a while, my mother had a revelation that God can protect you no matter what. So, we stayed in our home during the storm rather than panicking and fleeing, and our faith became stronger.

As I have stated, the foundation of my AM began early, living on Jim River. I remember that flowing river that reminded me of the positive flow of life. I can still see it today, moving around the rocks, as well as the beautiful scenery of nature and the stillness and calmness of a bright day. I still remember the powerful connection I had with my grandmother, a pillar of faith, strength, and influence. I remember the hopes and dreams of my mother for us to do well and contribute to the lives of others. I remember listening to the rain falling on the roof made out of tin. I remember the dusty roads and only being able to identify who was waving at you after the dust settled. I remember the white snow that covered the ground in winter.

During one particular instance, while driving, I remember being in awe of the sunset; it was so beautiful, powerful, and full of light and warmth. I have experienced the same while driving to work—the sun rising in its glory. When I see the sun, I think about our powerful God and Creator.

While visiting Maui, Hawaii, I was blessed and amazed to see vibrant and profound rainbows throughout the day. On the coast of California, where I often visit the massive ocean, I enjoy seeing the beautiful waves moving and flowing around the rocks. I have also seen the beautiful, colorful rocks and moonstones that the ocean gives back at low tide on the shore. Listening to the ocean helps me to become recalibrated by the ocean's voice and power, as well as the roar of the water and the waves.

As you can see, I have many Alabaster Moments and special experiences. I encourage you to embrace the philosophy of Alabaster Moments, of the joining together of alabaster (a precious mineral) to moments (points in time) to create an encounter that will carve, shape and heal your life. It is a process to begin transformation and healing in your life.

Chapter 12

AHA MOMENTS

"We cannot solve problems with the kind of thinking we employed when we came up with them."

– Albert Einstein

Alabaster Moments is about joyful, peaceful "aha" moments and experiences that shape our lives significantly, as well as our identity and the way we walk through the world. The definition of an "aha" moment is a point in your life—a time, event, or experience—when an important insight, choice, or decision is made. It can be comparable to when an audience moves toward empathizing with the main character when the emotional connection happens. And that is what gets an audience hooked. Alabaster Moments refers to mental enlightenment of, or insight into a problem or mystery; to a correct and deep understanding of someone or something; to the act or process of being aware of something for the first time.

AHA moments are:

- Anchored and felt from the core
- A wellspring of life
- Simply amazing
- Marvelous things
- Moments that exist peacefully in nature
- An unexpected gift
- Anchored in the beauty of nature
- Beautiful sunset

Chapter 13

KNOW YOUR WORTH

Remind Yourself of Your Value

"Stay away from those people who try to disparage your ambitions. Small minds will always do that, but great minds will give you a feeling that you can become great too."

– Mark Twain

The mind of God exists within us. It is the intuitive, expert mind that silently lets us know our worth, that we are free and moldable, just like the precious mineral, alabaster. We have free will to shape and design our lives. We can set up our moments in life. If our choices and experiences cause our shape to alter, we can go back on the potter's wheel and our wise "God mind" can help us create again. God is the designer of our worth and the silent whisper who reminds us of our worth. The Spirit is our navigator. He is the GPS that is perfect and absolute—if we listen to it.

The philosophy of AM is about knowing that you can recreate and mold your life by being intentional and setting up those utopian spaces where everything is ideal and perfect. In order to begin on the path of AM, we must focus on where our energy is going. Is it going in the direction of thinking about bad experiences that usually consume us and shape our lives in a way that makes us stuck in a loop of talking about the dreadful things that we have experienced? Let us choose to redirect our thinking, our focus, away from these bad experiences and toward the positive ones.

Have you ever noticed repeated numbers showing up on a clock, a sign on the road, a street number, etc.? One of my favorite angel numbers is the number 1111. It is said to be a call to action, asking you to align your thoughts and actions with your highest good and best self. Let us begin right now to align with our best selves.

You may ask, how do we know our best self, as it has been so long since we have seen it? To that, I respond, how would you describe your best self? What does it mean to you to experience good moments? How would you describe a good moment, and what words would you use? Some people name good moments as placid, quiet, serene, still, and untroubled.

Chapter 14

THE UNIVERSE SPOKEN INTO EXISTENCE

"When you change your thoughts, remember to also change your world."

– Norman Vincent Peale

Each of us has powerful testimonies that can help others breathe easier and find their way back to alignment and to healing and bouncing back quickly. Our testimony helps us to heal and have more compassion towards others, strengthening our spiritual path and living according to the divine plan that God has established for us.

Speaking over Your Life

When I speak of speaking over your life, I mean affirming love, hope, and positivity. When we speak over our lives, we are making a declaration of what we want to see manifest in our lives and releasing positive affirmations.

What do you speak over your life: negative words that become poisonous mist or positive words that are like an aromatic perfume, lifting our mood and helping us to feel better? An account in the Bible that resuscitates my soul is about Joseph, who interpreted dreams. Joseph had experienced being placed in prison, but he continued to use his precious gift by interpreting the king's dreams. By speaking over the lives of the king and of the people in the kingdom, Joseph drew in positivity and goodness.

Using our spiritual gifts encourages us to work together for the greater good. As we use our gifts and answer our calling, we can set up and deliver life-changing solutions and strategies for spiritual renewal, for individuals feeling overwhelmed. I use my philosophy of Alabaster Moments as a process for life growth and transformation. In striving for harmony in our lives, AM rekindles and maintains a positive flow of a vibrant life force.

Give from a Place of Love

I affirm that I will give and sow this book into the lives of others. I will offer this book as a gift of transformation to the world. I am releasing my thoughts on Alabaster Moments to the world.

The seed of AM has been planted in my spirit for many years. Seeds grow and scatter where many can reap and share in their harvest. As you know, a plant goes through several stages of growth, from a seed to a sprout, then through vegetative, budding, flowering, and ripening stages. I want you to share in the harvest of Alabaster Moments.

I remember as a child listening to music in the church. The song that ministered to my heart conveyed: "You cannot beat God, the Creator's giving. No matter how hard you try and just as sure as you are living. The more you give, the more He gives to you. But keep on giving because it is really true. That you cannot beat God's giving, no matter how you try." As you know, Alabaster Moments is about giving yourself great moments. The most potent great moments do not cost very much, like watching a mighty ocean, seeing a beautiful sunset, walking in the woods or the rain, riding in a car, seeing the beauty of the wildflowers, feeling the sunshine on your face, eating cold green grapes or tasty barbecue.

Deuteronomy 8:7-8 is a passage that further explains Alabaster Moments. It says that God is bringing you into a good land, a land of brooks of water, of fountains and springs, flowing forth in valleys and hills, a land of wheat and barley, of vines and fig trees and pomegranates, a land of olive oil and honey.

Chapter 15

WORDS ARE LIKE MEDICINE

Language is very powerful. Language does not just describe reality. Language creates the reality it describes.

– Desmond Tutu

The Power of Words is Like Medicine

I have come to realize that words create and describe moments. They create a feeling in which we reflect and think of those moments. Proverbs 15:4 says, "Gentle words bring life and health; a deceitful tongue crushes the spirit." Proverbs 20:15 speaks about wise speech as being rarer and more valuable than gold and rubies. Proverbs 18:4 says, "A person's words can be life-giving water; words of true wisdom are as refreshing as a bubbling brook."

All this is to say that what we hear with our hearts and think in our minds definitely plays a major part in our lives. The mind is one of the most powerful things, but it can be rigid and stop the flow of life. The mind can also deceive us sometimes and distort our thinking.

Consider the state of flowing that I mentioned earlier, in which I compare that state to water. Just as water always finds its way, so too must we find our way. We must get to a place where we are living from our higher self. We must be intentional in speaking positively over our lives, by producing and using kind words to ourselves and others. It is so rewarding to focus on positive experiences, appreciate small victories, find ways to be encouraged, and seek clarity on what a fulfilled life means. It is so important to define moments to help us rise and to think about what we are embracing in life.

When we embrace the divine, self-restoration begins. Restoration can bring delightful moments and nurture our souls. It is important to search to find the spark that ignites and revives our lives. It is important to build our lives around life-giving strategies to allow the good to flow like water.

Powerful quotes for reflection by the poet Rumi:

"The wound is the place where the Light enters you."

"Stop acting so small."

"What you seek is seeking you."

"Yesterday, I was clever, so I wanted to change the world. Today, I am wise, so I am changing myself."

"If you are irritated by every rub, how will your mirror be polished?"

"When you do things from your soul, you feel a river moving in you, a joy."

"Raise your words, not voice. It is rain that grows flowers, not thunder."

"Silence is the language of God, all else is poor translation."

"Be grateful for whoever comes, because each has been sent as a guide from beyond."

Powerful quotes for reflection by Hafez:

"Love is simply creation's greatest joy."

"Light will someday split you open; even if your life is now a cage."

"For we have not come here to take prisoners or to confine our wondrous spirits, but to experience ever and ever more deeply our divine courage, freedom, and light!"

Chapter 16

SACRED SCRIPTURE FOR RENEWAL

We are made for loving. If we do not love, we will be like plants without water.

– Desmond Tutu

When we fill our minds and hearts with God's word, we become aware of and familiar with His promises, which reside in our hearts. God promises to take care of our needs, protect us, strengthen us, and free our spirits from heaviness. The following passages from the Bible fill my heart with love and with God's messages.

John 10:10b sends a glorious message: "I am come that they might have life, and that they might have it more abundantly." "More abundantly" means to have greater abundance of a thing. An abundant life refers to life in its abounding fullness of joy and strength for the spirit, soul, and body.

Ecclesiastes 8:15 NIV states: "So, I commend the enjoyment of life, because there is nothing better for a person under the sun than to eat and drink and be glad. Then joy will go with them in their toil all the days of the life God has given them under the sun."

Also Isaiah 61:1 says: "The Spirit of the Lord God is upon me; because the Lord hath anointed me to speak good tidings unto the meek; he hath sent me to bind up the brokenhearted, to proclaim liberty to the captives, and the opening of the prison to them that are bound.

And, Acts 17:28 declares: "For in him we live and move and have our being."

From Psalm 118:24: "This is the day that the Lord has made; let us rejoice and be glad in it."

From Numbers 6:24-26: "The Lord bless you and keep you; the Lord make his face to shine upon you and be gracious to you; the Lord lift up his countenance upon you and give you peace."

From 2 Corinthians 9:11: "You will be enriched in every way to be generous in every way, which through us will produce thanksgiving to God."

Finally, from Psalm 95:2: "Let us come into his presence with thanksgiving; let us make a joyful noise to him with songs of praise!"

Remember that there is power in speaking positive words, particularly Scripture, over your life.

Live in Wellness!

My spirit speaks through this book to help others live in wellness. I have lived a life of providing support, guidance, and care to others for over twenty-five years, which has helped encourage me as well.

After all, throughout life, we have many beautiful experiences, yet somehow, we get fixated on difficult and awful moments. Oftentimes, our focus is on the things that have upset us, and we become stuck in that same loop that we cannot get out of, disenabling us from moving forward with joy. They become our focus and take up all the room in our minds, creating weeds that strangle our joy. Joy is then repelled and incapable of entering our lives, and if it does enter, we are not aware; it goes undetected.

I ask that you become a blank canvas and begin again right now, right where you are, regardless of the situation. Start the process to re-canvas and paint your life with beautiful moments. Focus on shifting your cognitive process and creating a beautiful masterpiece, beginning with your thinking.

You often hear the expression of thinking out of the box. Image the box is made of alabaster and image you break the box open. Now, visualize the change that is occurring in your life: You are speaking differently; your life is transformed; your walk is transformed, and your mind is transformed.

The breaking of the box has led to a release and to your life being filled with good and positive thoughts. Use Alabaster Moments to add big moments to your life. AM is about refocusing yourself to really enjoy moments in life.

We know that many things have happened to people such as abuse, the loss of loved ones, the loss of a job, the loss of our physical health, the loss of our mental health, the loss of our home, and the loss of who we are.

Alabaster Moments is about focusing not on these moments, but on those that have given us meaning in life. It may be the smell of pies that your grandmother was baking or a warm cup of cinnamon tea. It may be walking through the woods and picking berries, or planting flowers for a garden.

The creation of Alabaster Moments helps you focus and direct your energy on all the things that add value and hope to your life.

Finding Hope in Humble Beginnings

It has been said that words do not teach but experiences do. The value of lived experience is so potent, valuable, and informative. How you approach things in life creates either a negative vibration or a positive one.

Furthermore, we have an effect on each other because we are interconnected. So, we must keep a healing attitude, honor our breath, check our words and own our power to build, strengthen, and serve others. In spite of our current lot in life, we can begin again.

As you know, I grew up in humble beginnings, yet I found my AM in everyday encounters. I remember my mother was a housekeeper for a family. I loved when she would bring home their gently used clothing and items. I would become so excited and filled with gratitude that they were giving us all those wonderful things.

I have been thinking about wonderful moments like this for years. So now, these are my Alabaster Moments. I could have taken on the energy of feeling like I was not enough and like I was less than, but instead, I chose to feel gratitude and joy. Most people would probably say the items were junk, but I remember thanking God and could not wait to receive treasures again. I always reflect on this special Alabaster Moment.

The Spark of Hope

I would like to share a story to convey how God can do anything, and that what looks like the end can be a new beginning. On one particular day, my uncle had to go to the hospital. While there, he reported that he had died. He reported that he had risen up out of his body to the top of the room and could see the doctors wearing white coats working on his body on the table. He also shared with me that he heard one of the doctors ask if they should hit him again with the AED and one of the doctors responded, "What, hit him one more time with the defibrillator? He's dead." But another doctor said, "May as well hit him one more time." So, they did, and he started to come back to life and enter his body. My uncle lived for another ten years.

I remember as a young adult, always wanting to be close to God and wanting to experience His supernatural power, the miracles that I read about in the Bible, the faith and the strength that people carried and the great things they did. Every summer, the deacons from the church would come around and drive us to church so that we could develop a spiritual relationship with God. This process, called the mourner's bench, can be described as a rite of passage to connect and find meaning in God so that we can grow closer to Him.

Even then, that small voice was speaking to me, telling me to continue the rights of passage. But the first time the deacon picked me up and took me to a revival meeting—a meeting in which you seek God and, as a result, end up being baptized in the faith—I listened instead to the negative voice. I did not go back again to the church service.

When I was eighteen, another neighbor took me to a revival meeting. I have always carried such fear that my soul was already lost, that I had not followed the right path, and that it was not pleasing to God. But this time, I stuck it out.

On that particular night, the word of God was being preached and people were speaking about His goodness and power. Someone was speaking on the need to have God in your life. I pressed on through my fear and took the preacher's hand, and I said the words, "God has changed my life." As I walked to take the preacher's hand, I remember feeling fire go through my legs.

Prior to going to that service, I was reading the Bible, fasting, and praying. The Spirit had guided me to the account in the scripture in which a woman had an issue of blood but had faith in the healing power of God. This prepared me to walk out, guided by faith, and confess my belief in Jesus. That moment gave me hope for a better way for myself.

Life Choices

Make a list of the things that you want to incorporate into your life. If you are having difficulty moving forward, start by getting a large post-it and place it on the wall. Write at the top of the post-it, "Universe Please!" Think about the things that you are stuck with and having a hard time with. Write the things you want to carry out in life in the present tense.

For example, if the problems that have you stuck are:

- Lack of finances
- Living with fear
- Wanting a new job

You would write:

Universe Please!

I am so happy and grateful now that my finances are in divine order and overflowing in a good and positive way.

I am so happy and grateful now that my faith is strengthened.

I am happy and grateful now that I am at peace working at my new job.

The small voice we all have is the indicator that is trying to birth our purpose. The reason it never ignites is that we ignore it and do not act. The voice continues to send signals, but we do not respond. I made the mistake of not responding to that voice, but I eventually chose to accept what it was telling me.

We find our voice when we identify our strength and walk our path of truth. What we are passionate about helps our voice to come forth. We must have the discernment to know when to speak up and when not to speak up. Our voice drives our values in life. Our voice tells our story.

Chapter 17

LOOK INTO THE INTERIOR

"The most important person you meet in life is your higher self."

– Matshona Dhliwayo

Believe that God can do anything. Never count out God, our Creator. He has already given us the knowledge and the eternal blueprint. We must believe in Him and know that He has our backs. He will renew your mind, body, spirit, and heart from the inside out by helping you to act and build a transformative life through the creation of good, positive moments and experiences. He will give you moments that make you alive, that you can relive.

I remember hearing of the verse in the Bible in which Jesus calmed the storm. It reminded me of the home I grew up in, where there were fierce storms with high winds, thunder, and lightning. Although my family and I were very afraid, we were always protected and cared for each time it stormed.

Jesus said the Kingdom of God is like a farmer who scatters seeds on the ground. When seeds are planted, they grow to be something else. What I am conveying is that in life, we have to stop digging up what we have planted just because we are impatient. When we do that, we cut off our plant's growth. It is unable to fully take root, develop, and grow healthily. It is important to rest and let our seeds rest so that we can promote growth and create something strong.

You can begin to do better from right where you are currently in life.

The miraculous is within you. Your words and powerful mindset can create the very best. Words are power, and they grow into signs, miracles, and wonders.

You will see God's glory if you believe. Take heart in the following passages:

John 11:25 says: "I am the resurrection and the life." God can bless you out of all troubles.

Further, Matthew 12:34 says, "Out of the abundance of the heart, the mouth speaks." Renew the way you are speaking to create a new situation. Faith is always now. If we speak hope, we can feel hope and improve our situations in life.

I have God, who can do anything by my side. Know that He is setting me, and you up for a story. Erase the canvas of what your life looks like now and go to a place of hallelujah square for a new beginning. Hallelujah square is about release; letting go of the heaviness of your bondage and chains. It is about setting a continuous atmosphere of praise, speaking goodness, and trusting God. Can these dry bones live if you speak and prophesy life and good medicine?

Everything begins with the heart and the head. When we know what it is inside, we can stop reacting blindly and start living in abundance! Look inside your heart and be honest with yourself, and take time for an honest reflection. In our reflection, we become gracious, generous, and compassionate.

Chapter 18

WHAT COMES FROM THE HEART REACHES THE HEART

And now, here is my secret, a very simple secret: it is only with the heart that one can see rightly, what is essential is invisible to the eye.

– Antoine de Saint-Exupéry

Here is my secret:

The heart is powerful. It is the center of life, emotions, caring, and feelings. The Holy Book defines the heart as emotions and intellect. It says, "As a man thinks in his heart so is he. Above all else, guard your heart, for everything you do flows from it" (Pr. 4:23). It instructs us to **trust** in the Lord with all our heart and lean not on our own understanding (Proverbs 3:5).

Whatever we send to others, whether verbal or nonverbal, returns in like energy. A broken heart can stop us from living our most excellent life. Recall the example of the woman in the Bible that was living with an issue of blood. She sent a heartfelt message to Jesus that caused him to pause. This is an example of the idea that what comes from the heart touches the heart.

Alabaster Moments is a message from the heart for us to use our lives for enjoyable and memorable good times so that we can focus and dwell in joy and unity. I feel I have been called to bring this message from the heart to others. The original message spoken to me was to set up a process, purpose, and platform to open AM up to the world.

In my heart, I felt like this was not anything major; telling people to create and enjoy moments that mold them and give them a reference to help them when they are down. So, I had been in a period of non-action and waiting.

My heart says now is the time for the message of Alabaster Moments. For years, I have sent boxes filled with encouraging items to give others an Alabaster Moment when it is opened—similar to random acts of kindness and paying it forward. AM boxes are metaphorical, symbolizing the moment in the Sacred Book when the woman broke the box and changed the fragrance of the room. The room was also filled with forgiveness, hope, happiness, thoughtfulness, and bliss. It is my hope that when I send an AM box to someone, it changes the fragrance of their lives. Alabaster Moments can include the following:

A	Appreciation—an ability to understand the worth, quality, or importance of something, or the full awareness or understanding of something
L	Love—affection based on admiration, benevolence, or common interests
A	An "aha" moment—a moment of sudden realization, inspiration, insight, recognition, or comprehension
B	Being—the quality or state of having existence
A	Awakening—arousing from inactivity or indifference
S	Sensibility—awareness of and responsiveness toward something
T	Timelessness—having no beginning or end
E	Epiphany—a moment in which you suddenly see or understand something in a new or very clear way
R	Revelation—an act of revealing or communicating divine truth

Chapter 19

AWAKENING TO GRATITUDE

"Gratitude turns what we have into enough."

– Anonymous

Most of us are lost in a thick forest and cannot find gratitude. It is hidden from view, and many are unable to access the feeling of gratitude. When our focus and awareness are on painful circumstances, we operate in a frequency of feeling not good enough and not having enough. We consistently want more, but we are often stuck. So, how do we get out of this thinking?

Perhaps it would help for me to recall when I was trying to find a better way for myself. I was stuck in a loop of confusion, worry, anxiety, and uncertainty, and my dreams were hidden from view. During this time was when my father gave me that handful of change to travel many miles by bus all the way to San Francisco.

That was all he had to give me. Though most people would have looked down on the amount, I, however, embraced it fully. So, to answer the question of how to get out of negative thinking, the answer is this: gratitude is the checkpoint for forward momentum and change.

Having gratitude for even just a handful of change can lead to a world of growth and wonder. In life, it is important to look for situations to be grateful through faith, by practicing walking in gratitude, and not being led by the physical things that are happening.

Gratitude is recognizing and appreciating what you have and where you are in life, that things are as well as they are in the moment. It is so important to awaken to gratitude each day. Gratitude prepares us to receive more and provides a sacred space in our hearts to serve others.

I am so grateful for the wonderful memories of sitting on the porch with my mother, smelling the aroma of coffee as she drinks from her cup and uses witch hazel to refresh her face. I was in an environment of natural beauty with so much to be thankful for, such as those vibrant morning glory flowers. This was a marvelous way to start the day, spending time with myself and my mother.

It is so uplifting and informative to keep a gratitude journal of all your positive moments and to see the goodness in life. If we replace complaining with gratitude, our perspective begins to shift, which is such a refreshing feeling and brings such healing. Gratitude ushers in good and positive energy and the perfect environment for prosperity to enter your life and to stay in your life.

Chapter 20

MEDITATE ON GRATITUDE

"The goal of meditation is not to get rid of thoughts or emotions. The goal is to become more aware of your thoughts and emotions and learn how to move through them without getting stuck."

– Dr. P. Goldin

Alabaster Moments are about a peaceful and relaxed environment. My routine of meditation and gratitude begins early in the morning when I make space to burn incense and palo santo to awaken the senses, clear the space, and bring in new energy. I then sit in silence to see what comes up: if it is negative, I answer with a positive.

My gratitude list includes:

God	Food to eat	Abundance	Employment
Faith	Water to drink	Wealth	Friends
Power	Heart to give	Protection	Shelter
Ancestors	Prayer	Healthy mind	Clothing
My health	Compassion	Sunlight	Rain
Health of family	Activities of my limbs	Wisdom	Peace of Mind
My mother	House to live in	Positive outlook on life	Kindness
My father	Eyesight	Safety	Freedom

Sisters and brothers	Comfortable bed	Intelligence	Positive thoughts
Nieces and Nephews	New information	Spirituality	Relaxing
Aunts, uncles, and cousins	Happy moments	Passion	Purpose

Chapter 21

PHILOSOPHY OF TRANSFORMATION

I AM Alabaster

We are alabaster. We are made and shaped by the handiwork of God.

This book is about moments! I see positive moments as sparks in life. I see positive moments as a way to change our lives and transform. If we are continuously having bad moments, we can begin to set up better moments that help us find our way and change our lives. Moments are like water; they flow all the time. There, too, are key moments in life that help us to feel and think better, feel powerful, and enjoy beautiful experiences that change our lives.

The Alabaster Philosophy

Heart of AM Philosophy

The alabaster philosophy is that you come as you are with great expectation, knowing God can do anything. You hope for great possibilities, and what happens is that through your certainty, through your lack of hesitation, you are able to reach your destination of transformation.

It is a philosophy where you begin right where you are, and you start to affirm the positive and you begin to be mindful of your thinking because you know that thoughts become actions and become patterns in your lives. Alabaster Moments is about bringing back those moments that leave us in awe and amazement and allowing the positive to flow in our lives.

I have worked at an acute care behavioral health setting for fourteen years straight every weekend. Even though I was serving and providing great care to others, I had put my life on hold. In addition to working every weekend, I also worked a full-time job from Monday through Friday. My life was filled with so much busyness and ongoing tasks that I had to remember to get done. Everything seemed to be rushing too quickly. I noticed I was just operating and existing. I was not aware of any sacred moments in life. I was tired and exhausted with no time for myself. I did not consider moments of rejuvenation. Rather, I ignored them, and my purpose was lost in the chaos; I could not recall any wonderful moments that I was living.

This book is about appreciating and becoming aware of the power of positive, life-changing, and healing moments. There are many moments that define our current reality, but our lens are often focused on the negative, which lowers and crushes our spirit. Many verbalize that their lives have been filled with bad moments, which means that their eyes were not opened to see any good. If we were to think deeply, we would see that there are times that have occurred in life that have added valuable experiences.

Welcome to the wondrous world of Alabaster Moments and to the times of reflection that lead to your majestic rising, to you connecting to and embracing your divine self. Those restorative experiences that bring joy and delight to your life. The moments that nurture your soul, your mind, your will, and your emotions. The quiet sparks that ignite and revive your life, allowing the good to flow. The life-affirming and giving moments and instances that recreate positive energy and situations that enhance your life force and greatness.

Another way to define Alabaster Moments is to think of them as a special experience or point in time in which everything is intimately connected that changes the fragrance of life. Reflecting back on that time brings happiness, joy, and a great sense of serenity. It takes you to that place of calm where everything is in alignment and flow. It results in a coming together of the inner and outer mind, the body, and the spirit—a state of blessing.

Alabaster Moments is about starting to live life right now no matter the circumstances. When we practice being intentional, we can reflect on those flashes of awe. If you feel you do not have any positive moments in life, I encourage you to start now. Be intentional about setting up an atmosphere, an environment that nourishes and promotes healing and rejuvenation.

I encourage you to rediscover the importance of taking breaks in your life. Value the gift of being able to think worthy thoughts about yourself and others. Reflect on times that have added great value to your existence, that have improved your self-worth and self-esteem, and ushered in hope, optimism, healing, and peace. You can engage in simple practices that can help you focus and improve the life that you are living. It is important to adopt a mindset that flows into harmony, connecting the body and spirit.

Alabaster Moments is about opening our eyes to see those great, defining life moments. AM is needed to help spark that 'something' in us so that we may begin to carve the life we want. When we begin to carve our lives, it starts a rebirthing, no matter what we are going through right now. We have the choice to choose and add better moments to our lives.

It is my desire that this book heals, recharges, and touches lives from generation to generation. I believe in sacred divine experiences and realize those instants heal, protect, and supply a safe place.

I welcome you to the wondrous magical world of Alabaster Moments, a return to sacred living. AM aligns with the timeless story in the Bible that birthed a story of transformation and new beginnings. It is a powerful moment in the Holy Sacred Scriptures which described the action of a woman who had been counted out. She was judged and not viewed as doing very positive things in life.

Does this sound familiar? Rather than becoming fixated on your troubles and staying in that negative place, I would like you to enter and create a world filled with the spirit of alabaster. That place is a peaceful place, a sacred place—a place of healing, restoration, and transformation.

Chance meetings can be sparks in life and are important because they shape and impact our lives. With this book, I want to encourage each of you to find this chance meeting using the metaphor of connecting the concepts of alabaster and moments and using that as a philosophy to create great life encounters and to hold them as sacred memories that promote life.

Alabaster Moments is about turning your storm into a story of transformation. It is about changing your environment, changing your name—either literally, figuratively, or both—and having a picture of your life that is pleasing to God. It is so important to speak from this place of desiring transformation.

It is important, too, to become familiar with the Bible which is a holy sacred book—a book that builds character and strength and gives hope and testimony of lived experiences as if they were happening right now.

I encourage you to:

- Find a quiet place
- Read the Bible daily
- Pray in the morning
- And at night prior to bed
- Create your own Alabaster Moments

MY Approach

My approach to transformation is helping others create Alabaster Moments. To create times that bring memories of joy, peace, serenity, safety, and security. It is important to seek a better way that helps us to feel better and cared for in life. It is so refreshing to see the beauty in times that give us a fresh outlook and a better perspective.

Alabaster Moments is an approach that when you embrace and enter that sacred space, you know things are going to get better. Your faith begins to stir in you and you start to realize the power that you have. A change in thinking begins and you begin to restore your identity and gain a new positive experience of hope, restoration, and rejuvenation. You no longer see things in your life as bad. The weight has lifted, and your thinking and internal dialogue have changed to usher in the path that leads to a better way.

Practicing the Philosophy of Alabaster Moments

There are so many sacred gifts and holidays. When we practice the philosophy of Alabaster Moments, we live each day like it is a holy day or holiday.

When I hear the word "holy," I think of something that is good and perfect, a part of divine order and of doing good things. All is well in alignment.

When I think of peace, I think of internal peace, external peace, and eternal peace. I think about Jehovah Shalom, another name for God, our Creator. The name 'Jehovah' conveys the thought of being, or existing, or becoming known, while the term "shalom" refers to soundness, completeness, harmony, and the absence of strife. It is best rendered by our English word, peace.

Furthermore, the dove is often associated with peace, tranquility, and grace. Its meaning has become so universal that major world religions such as Christianity and Judaism have used the symbol as the truest representation of peace, grace, and divinity. A dove, or an olive branch, is often used as a symbol of peace. These are derived from the story of Noah in the Old Testament, which tells how, after a terrible flood that wiped out most human beings and animals, God made peace with humankind.

Incorporating peace daily requires starting our day by calling in peace through meditation, listening to inspirational music, reading, speaking positive words, and being present with God. Peace is about choosing what to focus on and invite into our life.

Chapter 22

CALLING IN THE EXTRAORDINARY

Think of the best, encouraging, memorable, unforgettable, extraordinary, remarkable moments in your life that have transformed your life. When you look back on these remarkable times, you feel joyful, soothed, and comforted. These are times that are defined by feeling free, safe, secure, and relaxed, and you want to repeat those points in time and recreate and relive those moments.

I often thought about the need for Alabaster Moments when I was working in an acute care setting where people had given up the will to live, had thoughts to hurt themselves and others, and felt unsafe. My career has been in what is referred to as the healing arts. I have worked with the broken, depressed, sad, helpless, and hopeless, and those in need of recovery. They are lost and unable to support themselves and embrace who they truly are.

Working as a psychotherapist, I started to hear from the spirit, a powerful call to action. I am introducing AM to the world tell others to open their eyes, pause, and create moments that will help them. Out of the twenty-four hours in the day, we can begin to take just five to fifteen minutes to align with a better feeling.

Chapter 23

THE MOLDING OF ALABASTER MOMENTS

"The higher goal of spiritual living is not to amass a wealth of information, but to face sacred moments."

– Rabbi Abraham Joshua Heschel

"Let yourself be silently drawn by the strange pull of what you really love. It will not lead you astray."

– Rumi

Everyone has experienced at least one Alabaster Moment. Alabaster Moments begins with reimagining a better way of walking through life and being in a nurturing place in the world. I believe that reintroducing positive moments and experiences in life creates a lifeline to build upon and reset the mind, body, and spirit.

The greatest AM is Christmas. It is a time filled with an explosion of wonders and memorable moments. During the Christmas season, there is an atmosphere of carving out the hardness from our hearts, making us happier and more open to giving and receiving.

Another way to understand Alabaster Moments is to think about going away to a beautiful hotel or resort. It is nice, neat, and clean. Everything is organized and in the right place. It is full of beautiful luxurious things such as plush, soft linen; comfortable, nice, soft bed sheets; and soothing hot and cold beverages like water, juices, coffee, and tea. There are beautiful pictures on the wall in the bathroom, the towels are soft, and the body wash, soap, and shampoo are so creamy, fragrant, and uplifting. The hotel has the finest of things: beautiful scenery, a positive, uplifting, friendly atmosphere, people filled with kindness, wonderful conversations, and an environment of connecting and enjoying life.

Alabaster Moments encompass those defining moments in life that you want to relive. They are the moments that restore the feeling of possibility and not only make you feel great but also help you understand life as worth living.

If we can see with the eyes of the Spirit and experience His sacredness, we can reframe our life. When we change how we see life, in that moment, we start appreciating, and we turn fragmented or broken pieces of life into building blocks that become ladders of gratefulness.

What are some moments you can begin to think about setting up intentionally? It does not matter if you are going through painful moments in life, such as health problems, the loss of a job, having to change locations, or not having a lot of money. You can still set up Alabaster Moments even if it is just by slicing lemon or adding mint to a glass of water. Simple things can be soothing, like taking a walk and noticing the beautiful wildflowers.

The purpose of AM is to form and shape your life to feel happy and great. When we are in perfect alignment, we model the divine, which brings alignment with our:

- Purpose
- Courage
- Value
- Release
- Action
- Pouring
- Anointing
- Upgrading
- Transforming

An article published in the *Journal of Psychology of Religion and Spirituality* details a study in which 2,889 participants were asked about the frequency with which they generally experience "sacred moments" in their everyday lives. Individuals were instructed to rate, on a scale of 1 (never/not at all) to 5 (very often), how often they experience:

- "a moment that felt set apart from everyday life,"

- "a moment…that was really real,"

- "a moment in which all distractions seemed to melt away,"

- "a deep sense of connection with someone or something,"

- "a sense of uplift," and

- "a sacred moment."

According to the study, having sacred moments in your life can lead to better mental health. Individuals who experienced sacred moments predicted higher levels of positive emotions and a greater presence of meaning in their lives. They also experienced lower levels of perceived stress, distress, depression, and anxiety.

As you can see, sacred moments can be Alabaster Moments, and they can mold and shape our lives.

Chapter 24

BENEFITS OF ALABASTER MOMENTS

These moments can help us when we are feeling down, broken, or defeated, and when we cannot find our way. That is when we need a positive remembrance of experiences that restore joy. If we are unable to find those moments, we have to form those joyful moments to transform our way of feeling.

Alabaster Moments is about forming and upgrading our moments in life. It is about being intentional in setting up possibilities. It is not about waiting for something to happen or waiting until everything is perfect, but about finding and creating that moment for yourself.

AM is about noticing a beautiful environment or a beautiful location. And within that location is glorious beauty that fills you with the joy of simple living. AM can even be as simple as a freshly brewed cup of coffee or tea; the fragrance and taste of a sweet orange; or the feeling of soft, plush, soothing towels and warm water on the face. AM may be experienced in a delicious salad, a hot soup, and buttery bread.

Really, Alabaster Moments is a call to really start living.

Chapter 25

BREAKING OF ALABASTER

Remember that alabaster is a precious mineral that can be shaped, molded, and carved. A box made of alabaster is able to keep whatever is placed inside pure and unspoiled. The contents are sealed inside and have to be broken in order to be released. Imagine that you are made of alabaster, and you are pure and unspoiled inside. Think about your life and the moments that have shaped, molded, and carved your life and the life of others. When you are broken, what fragrance is released? Is it a fragrance of great moments of happiness, or is it pain, anger, frustration, and sadness? What if the broken pieces had messages of the following?

- Be intentional and speak positively over your life
- Use kind words to yourself and others
- Send out kind words and deeds to the world
- Respect and value the gift of life
- Give thanks for life
- Focus on positive experiences
- Focus on small victories
- Find ways to encourage yourself and others
- Seek clarity on what a fulfilled life means to you
- Define moments to help you rise
- Embrace your divine self

- Seek restoration by making choices to bring delight to yourself
- Choose moments that nurture your soul
- Find the spark that ignites and revives your life
- Build your life with amazing moments
- Focus on life-giving strategies
- Allow the good to flow in your life

There are many stories of alabaster that come to mind. Remember, Alabaster Moments starts with reimagining a better way of walking through and being in the world.

Stories

Special Olympics

I remember an AM that occurred at the Special Olympics. During a race, one of the runners tripped and fell. Everyone thought that he was done; they sighed and counted him out. But then he got back up. And not only did he get back up, he also ignited his strength and energy and raced past everyone, crossing the finish line in first place. In that second of defeat, his flame was restored within him. What a point in time to remember!

Attorney

While working as a mental health clinician, I met a client who was an attorney. She was not able to work because she had become unwell. She was feeling down and had lost her confidence. She learned a problem-solving technique in which she brainstormed her possibilities, evaluated the alternatives, assessed each option, and determined what she would follow through with to improve her problem. Thus, her motivation was rekindled and she returned back to her life's work as an attorney. She was derailed only for a moment.

Family Connection

I also worked with a young girl who was placed in a foster care home due to physical abuse from her mother. While conducting a home visit with her, I grew acquainted with the foster father in the home. I shared that I was originally from Louisiana, which I am very proud of. So, he informed me that he was also from Louisiana. He asked me who my people were, and I told him. He then shared that my great uncle's wife was his sister and that he had not seen her in twenty years. So, I reconnected them through a telephone call. This chance happening created an AM for them. They were able to talk, share stories, reconnect, and tell each other they loved and appreciated each other. They both were grateful.

Closed Hand

One of the most powerful lessons that was brought to my awareness was when my uncle demonstrated that when your hand is closed, nothing can get out, and nothing can get in; there is no flow and movement. If we want to receive better moments in life, we must be open to receive.

Resuscitation

Earlier, I share the story of my uncle and his near-death experience—the same uncle who told me about the closed hand. And so, when we have moments of alabaster, it transforms us and helps us to reach the light even in dark moments.

Chapter 26

MY ALABASTER STORY

As you know well by now, I grew up with modest beginnings, which many of us may have experienced. I would like to share with you how the Spirit gave me my Alabaster Moments.

Memories

Many memories shape my alabaster path. I can remember drawing water out of a cistern to drink and wash clothes. I can remember not being able to walk through the front door of the house because the porch needed repair. I can remember being able to open the gate because we lived in a field—a pasture where animals were also behind the gate. I can remember dusty roads and no pavement. I can remember looking across the road in front of our house and seeing a cotton field. I can remember that when the really bad electrical storms came, we would run from our small little house to my aunt's house for refuge. I can remember my brother hunting for birds and roasting them in the fireplace for us to eat. I can remember placing sweet potatoes in the fireplace to roast. I can remember capturing the rainwater so that we could have drinking water. I can remember my grandmother having to churn and turn milk into butter.

These are some of the many Alabaster Moments along my journey that I share with you.

Chapter 27

TOOLS OF ALABASTER MOMENTS

"The wound is the place where the Light enters you."

– Rumi

Everyone has some difficulty with trust because fear is so easily stirred up and can overpower and consume us. Fear can derail us from having powerful moments in life. I have heard over and over in the church that fear is referred to as false evidence that appears real. Fear places us in a situation of pause and uncertainty and interrupts our life. Fear further presses down our small inner voice and causes the whisper to become very faint.

Everyone needs to hear new perspectives to open their awareness to learning and receiving truth and knowledge. We all have power within if we are able to listen to it. When I begin to experience feelings of fear, I call out to infinite wisdom and intelligence, asking for guidance to show me the way.

Also, the power of breathing helps to reset the mind, body, and spirit. Breathing has many benefits, such as calming the body down, helping us to manage stress, giving the body vital energy, and helping our body to receive sufficient life force.

Love, faith, and alignment are key factors and very important in our life. Love is unconditional and changes the heart. As we love ourselves continually, we become familiar and comfortable with the feeling power and benefits of love. Love helps us to trust life and believe that life is for us. Love helps us to share our life with others.

Faith is an essential tool for healing; it brings forth self-confidence, strong belief, and security. The spirit of fear can spread very fast, causing individual and collective panic, but there is strength in believing by faith.

Alignment helps our spirit to stay strong and connected to healthy positive energy. When we are feeling down, usually our energy is low and needs to be recharged.

If we are going to mold and carve our lives, we are going to need some tools. We could all benefit from having a toolkit designed for our growth in life, to help us carve out sustainable moments and restore our strength.

Tools help to improve self-esteem and self-acceptance, restore our ability to relax and feel connected, as well as foster a sense of belonging.

Helpful Tools and Strategies

Meditation	It is a process of emptying the mind of all clutter. When you empty the mind of clutter, you are open to more possibilities.
Labyrinths	The labyrinth is used for spiritual centering, contemplative prayer, and reflection of spiritual questions. It helps with quieting the mind, calming anxiety, recovering balance, enhancing creativity, and encouraging insight and self-reflection. The labyrinth helps us to focus on our inner world. It can be a physical metaphor for the journey we are traveling in life.

Mandala	The mandala is representative of the center and circle of life. There are many circles in life: our earth, the world, the universe, and wholeness. The mandala can be very beneficial in helping to relax the mind, body, and spirit. It is also a tool of self-expression as it helps us to discover our deep, inner truth and what lies in our unconscious. When the mind, body, and spirit are relaxed, feelings of happiness, inner peace, and well-being are evoked. When we are feeling well, we are less stressed, our anxiety is reduced, we worry less, and our feeling of being overwhelmed goes away. That way, we can focus on our purpose and that which gives us meaning in life. When we are in a chaotic psychological state, this tool helps us to discover ways to release and heal.
Positive Affirmations	Positive statements about what we want to carry out: My good comes to me in infinite ways. Unexpected and magical surprises show up each day. I look in wonder at that which shows up for me. I am harmonious and glow with radiance. My happiness is built upon infinite wisdom. Eternity has given me a story of beauty.

Journaling	Journaling helps us to think better and see our patterns of thinking.
	So, we can process our thoughts and feelings.
	It helps us to gain valuable self-knowledge.
	Journaling helps to process and release emotions.
	It engages both hemispheres of the brain and improves cognitive functioning.
	It strengthens the immune system, preventing a host of diseases.
	It counteracts many of the negative effects of stress.

Tools for Your Toolkit

Affirmations for comfort

Listening to inspiring music

Using information to help increase awareness and truth

Writing in a journal

Brewing a warm cup of tea or coffee

Appreciating the gift of life

Speaking to someone you trust

Talking to a friend

Enjoying beautiful flowers

Relaxing in nature

Using lotion with an essential oil such as lavender

Meditating on positive moments of good

Opening our hearts and minds to receive good

Marvelous, unexpected good/victories

Entering into bliss and goodness

Nurturing the Soul and feeling good

Listening to the ocean

Taking time to restore the good

Seeing life as good

Chapter 28

CONNECTING TO GOD

"Remember God so much that you are forgotten. Let the caller and the called disappear; be lost in the Call."

– Rumi

As a child, I learned the importance of the Bible. I was taught to read the Bible because it would help me live life better. I was taught I could learn the essence of God. So, I tried to read the Bible. Sometimes I would lose interest and try again when I was going through problems and situations.

I remember feeling very peaceful when reading the Bible. I had feelings that messages were coming forth to help me that helped me think better and solve my problems. I could feel the heaviness of life situations get lighter when reading the Bible. The Bible, most importantly, helped me to understand the importance of connecting to the power of God. When we connect with God, we can understand His attributes. The attributes of God are eternal, gracious, holy, loving, infinite, independent, good, and cannot change.

Reading the accounts in the Bible fortifies my soul and balances my spirit. I can remember how my faith was built up, strengthened, and restored when reading the Bible, praying, and just being, listening in silence for a two-week period. I could hear the voice of God speaking to my spirit, building my faith and restoring my soul.

I understand that life can be mysterious, but if we seek to be aware of God's presence, we will see that He communicates with us constantly and His guidance is true. In fact, dreams are prophetic visions and conversations that give us guidance and revelations. Even through a dream, God is telling us to speak or act. The Sacred Book, too, speaks about writing a vision and making it plain.

Listening to God

"Sit quietly and listen for a voice that will say, 'Be more silent.' As that happens, your soul starts to revive."

— **Rumi**

When we listen and tune into the voice of God, we build a relationship with God, a connection to His blessings and promises. The Bible helps us to gain knowledge, guidance and understanding of life through His voice.

There are many advantages to listening to God. When we listen to Him, He fills us with His peace, presence, and love. When we feel at peace, we can relax, think good thoughts, and operate in calmness. When we listen to God, our vision for our lives is shaped and we receive clarity through His instructions.

What is your vision for your life? Reflect back and think about the times in your life that you have received and felt positive praise. Are you working within your identified life purpose? Have you ever set up a goal in your life? What is your gauge for doing well and how do you measure it? What purpose stirs your soul, motivates you, and brings unspeakable great joy to your life? Are you tuned into the Spirit who brings abundant life? What is needed for you to go from declaring to doing? This is achieved by running in tune with your purpose and spiritual path.

AM is my inspired vision from God. It came out of me listening and being obedient to His instructions. AM is about being connected to great moments in time. The goal is to align memories with your vision for your life. In working wholeheartedly, we must always put God first and always return to the sacred.

I encourage you to live great moments each day of your life. Use as a reference the accounts in the Bible that are very helpful for healing and supplying medicine for the weary and restless soul.

The soul of the diligent is richly supplied. Only your purpose and faith in God will stand. The Bible shows that we are to be respectful and be positive, hopeful models, living and teaching dignity and integrity. God has given us all the power of being able to love. The spreading of love helps the mind, body, spirit, community, and world.

Chapter 29

CONNECTING WITH SPIRIT FOR REBUILDING

I am and continue to be dedicated to providing support to help individuals facing a variety of life issues. I have brought up in no uncertain terms the number of people who seem to be out of alignment with their true divine spirit; who seem to have low energy, who seemed to be overwhelmed by negative thinking.

I have seen the importance of restoring a negative spirit through my many years of supplying care and service. I would say that it is highly important to act quickly and promptly when your spark is starting to go out. It is important to turn the spark into a flame, into a fire of passion and purpose, and to live with vitality.

I remember receiving a telephone call for therapeutic service and care. I was asked if I provided care to people dealing with obsessive-compulsive disorder. While listening to the request, I informed that maybe it was best to look for more of a specialty mental health service. I informed that I provided care to individuals experiencing mild to moderate issues. After the explanation, I was asked to set up an appointment for further assessment. When meeting for this assessment, it became clear that the person was in complete distress and fully out of alignment, just like the woman in the Bible with the alabaster box.

I guided the individual to take steps towards recovery by:

- Having purpose within the heart

- Entering the room with courage

- Activating release

- Carrying within themselves the valuable

- Deciding to get care for their situation and actively entering the room to receive it

- The ultimate goal is to upgrade the atmosphere and create a story of transformation.

In my professional work with clients, I have found that it is important to provide a safe, nurturing, welcoming, and therapeutic environment. When the environment is safe, nonjudgmental, and filled with hope and optimism, healing and recovery can begin.

It is important to allow the client to share their story to begin reconnecting to their purpose in life. Many times, motivation has grown weak, and they need to recall positive life experiences to begin again. A primary focus is to develop trust, be empathetic, and listen for insight and growth.

Listening and identifying strategies to help the client act as catalysts for transformation. In the process of transformation, new strength and courage begin to evolve, which brings powerful insight and helps with taking action. The learning and application of new techniques can help the client to begin to elevate their areas of thinking, motivation, self-confidence, and problem-solving.

So now, I want you to consider these: how do you restore your spark? What are some ways to restore your spark?

- Sit in silence and listen

- Listen for any thoughts of instruction that come to your mind

- Listen to what comes to your mind in terms of feedback

- What is the connection between the thoughts that you are thinking and the life that you are living?

- Evaluate the thoughts and the silent feedback that you have received

- Take simple steps of action

- Focus on one action per week

- Track in a journal your journey and any progress

- Evaluate how your internal spirit is feeling and evolving

- Restore your alignment

Chapter 30

THE WAY TO MY LEGACY

"You have no idea what your legacy will be because your legacy is every life you touch."

– Maya Angelou

The pathway to my legacy has been paved by the Great Spirit of Life. I am always filled with amazement, admiring the wonder of God, our Creator. The Great Spirit of Life is the first visionary, trendsetter, and innovator.

The book of Genesis, which means the original, shows the power of speaking words. When we speak, we create and build a place to exist for ourselves, just like how the Great Spirit spoke the earth into existence. I think we are all familiar with the way that God created the earth, especially those well-known words, "Let there be light."

And through his words and actions, God made us in his image. As such, I realize that I am a representative of God. I, like God, am wisdom, understanding, counsel, fortitude, knowledge, and devotion—as are you.

It is my desire to leave a legacy of light and illumination for others, to restore light and rekindle the flame in the lives of all that I meet. I would like my earthly calling to mirror and reflect God and help others to create a life that is pleasing to God, a life that is inclusive of God. A life that does not ignore God but puts him first in all that we do, say, and believe.

I would like to call forth a legacy of freedom, joy, and liberation for people. I would like a legacy of setting the captives free so that they can live abundantly and be a light to others. I want to leave a message, blueprint, and a spiritual global positioning system that supplies light to others and guides them in their metamorphosis and leads to greatness. I want to leave a legacy of powerful impact that helps others to breathe easier and live to the fullest so that they can have a life of continuous humility, growth, and transformation. I will plant the seeds from generation to generation with the spoken and written word of the molding power of Alabaster Moments.

May the words of my mouth and the meditations of my heart be forever acceptable to God.

Chapter 31

A PLACE OF HEALING

Everyone needs a safe, secure space to reflect, think, heal, and restore their energy. We all need a structure and routine to clear and replenish our minds and heal from the ravages of chaos

I encourage those who are hurting, broken, confused, and counted out to focus on better moments and finding that place of renewal. After all, our use of our energy is very important when we feel down and we are in need of a place and plan of renewal; it is important to find that place.

In life, there are many places where we can restore and heal. It may be a cabin in nature, a hotel on the beach or ocean, a trip to a resort area, a walk in the woods, or a hike up a hill. It can be going to the park, awakening to the sunrise, hearing the rain, seeing a rainbow, or having a cup of coffee or tea.

CONCLUSION

Growing up as a child, I began to understand the power of the right information. One day, a lady came to our house to tell us about a program for learning called Head Start. I was young and really did not know what it was until she showed up again, supplying transportation, and took me and my brother to the program.

I began to learn so many things and my world began to expand. The learning increased my awareness, my view of the world, and opened my belief in education and learning. I have always believed in learning because it ignited my imagination. I believe, as Albert Einstein said, 'imagination is more powerful than knowledge.' I believe that learning, knowledge, and moments are the catalyst for being able to imagine and create.

I used these beliefs as a young woman living in San Francisco, California. In trying to find a better way, I was open and eager to learn anything that would make my life better. So, too, do I hope you are able to take lessons from this book and learn.

While cleaning and sorting through a closet full of old items and junk, I found a little, old, dusty red book that was ripped with the pages falling out. The title of the book was *The Game of Life and How to Play It* by Florence Scovel Shinn. I almost tossed the book away without looking inside just based on its physical appearance, but something made me read it.

And as I did, I got so connected to the book because it brought forth pertinent information for me. The information transformed my way of thinking. It transformed how I viewed life. It helped me to reduce my stress and to notice what words I was speaking, what thoughts I was thinking, and what ways I was treating other people. The book caused me to pause and sent me on a journey of applying what I had learned in the book to my real-life experiences.

The book shaped my reality in a very positive manner and contributed to my approach to helping and serving others. It, and the moments that have come about as a result, has been an important building block for my life and for how I provide support to others. So here is some of the information I learned on that day:

- The greatest of knowledge and insight can be included in something that is viewed as torn, worn, useless, and meant to be thrown away.

- Just because something is falling apart or torn and is no longer new does not mean it does not have value.

- There are hidden treasures waiting to be discovered that can transform your life and the many lives of others.

Also, the book helped me to understand the power of words and how they are creators in life. And not to despise the "day of small things," as just because things are small does not mean they have less value or benefit. My favorite affirmations that the book inspired in me are:

"Infinite Spirit, open the way for my right home, my right friend, my right position. I give thanks it now manifests under grace in a perfect way."

"I am Alabaster. I am made and shaped by the handiwork of God."

Remember what alabaster is—a mineral that can be molded and holds that which is valuable. Remember that a moment is a point in time. When the two come together, you have a sacred encounter or moment—Alabaster Moments.

For many years I have, supplied services and support for individuals who are unable to feel joyful, who focus on all the bad that has happened, whether past or present, who engage in negative thinking.

This book is for them, and for you. It will help you to take current inventory of your life moments and become intentional about setting time for recharging, rather than allowing difficult moments to consume your life and bring you down.

Begin creating your Alabaster Moments now.

POURING OF ALABASTER:

POETIC EXPRESSIONS

A- All is Well!

Something happened to me

That shook the inner part of me

I struggled just to be

I went in the four corners of my mind

Trying to be free

I became frustrated

I got overwhelmed

The fear was overrated

But I could not take it

It was like receiving a bad letter

In the mail

It was like a story

With no ending

That I could tell

I revived my mind

Improved the condition

Over time

Gave my life the benediction

All is well!!!

L-Live Bright

Walking through the earth

I stay strong so I can ignite
Understand that I am a Light
I have power to illuminate
Brighten up the night
I am a day star

Shining so bright
I stay strong and anchored

In my power
Commanding with might
I am smooth like water
A nonresistant stream

There is no fight
Filled with powerful spiritual energy
Stirring up my dreams
I reside in the overflow

Connecting earth to the heavenly

Radiating the light

I live bright

A- Atmosphere

It is time to change

The atmosphere

To shake up the status quo

To find that healing flow

To usher in positive energy

To release a beautiful fragrance

To stir up the spirit of synergy

So, I can have a fair chance

To feel the energy of hope

By breaking the boxes

That restrict and contain

Like a yoke

My mind, body, and spirit

That keep creating a familiar dance

A continuous cycle

That blocks my chance

To get in the healing stream

Leaving me left out

Unredeemed

B-BELIEVE

Believe in the energy

That elevates you higher

The moments that fill

You with passion and desire

Hold tight to the good

Eliminate the shoulds

Go inward and deep

Nourish the points in time

You would like to keep

Remove all doubt

Take actions that relieve

Plug into the powerhouse of good

Believe

A-Amazement

God's creation is beautiful

So very captivating

We must eliminate the hate

It is devastating

The earth and the people

Are divine and royalty

But they are stuck

Having eyes but cannot see

Believing in the wrong truth

Not knowing what is up

They have downloaded

A letter of resentment

Without inner proof

Within is a bitter cup

In need of a healing portion

To feel relieved

And bring elation
So they can rise
In amazement

S- Suddenly

My world has changed

Things are happening to me

That I cannot explain

It came upon me

All of a sudden

It looks like the universe

Just pushed a magic button

But I am stuck

My spirit cannot receive

My thoughts still deceive

I know that everything

Is within arm's reach

It is so hard

To believe

That things have changed

My life has been rearranged

I walk different

I think different

I am brand new

Suddenly

I can finally be

T- This Too Shall Pass

My mind worries all the time

It is like a clock with a fast chime

I try to refocus

Think of something new

The energy gets so intense

I do not know what to do

My mind is filled with what ifs

Moving so fast

I met a spiritual teacher

Who told me

Things are never as bad

As they seem

The sun will rise

New mercies every day

Troubles do not last

This too shall pass

E-ENERGY

Pay close attention

To your energy

It flows and attracts

It repels and reacts

It is within and without

It is all you got

To help you vibrate higher

To stir up

That fire in life

Without it

You pay a high price

You may find yourself in the valley

Unable to rise

Like attracts like

Align with your life force

Find powerful motivation to be

Stir up your positive energy

R-REVIVED

In life I have tried

To secure and receive the prize

Something within me

Is holding me back

Weighing my ability down

Dimming the lights in my crown

I need a closer

Walk with thee

To restore the true me

The wrong has to come out

Rise to the top

To make me feel free

And alive

SI can feel replenish and

Be revived

Made in the USA
Monee, IL
15 October 2023

44610186R00070